F. E. Bentley
Princeton
March 1967

REGENTS RENAISSANCE DRAMA SERIES

General Editor: Cyrus Hoy
Advisory Editor: G. E. Bentley

MICHAELMAS TERM

THOMAS MIDDLETON

Michaelmas Term

Edited by

RICHARD LEVIN

UNIVERSITY OF NEBRASKA PRESS · LINCOLN

Publishers on the Plains
UNP

MANUFACTURED IN THE UNITED STATES OF AMERICA

Regents Renaissance Drama Series

The purpose of the Regents Renaissance Drama Series is to provide soundly edited texts, in modern spelling, of the more significant plays of the Elizabethan, Jacobean, and Caroline theater. Each text in the series is based on a fresh collation of all sixteenth- and seventeenth-century editions. The textual notes, which appear above the line at the bottom of each page, record all substantive departures from the edition used as the copy-text. Variant substantive readings among sixteenth- and seventeenth-century editions are listed there as well. In cases where two or more of the old editions present widely divergent readings, a list of substantive variants in editions through the seventeenth century is given in an appendix. Editions after 1700 are referred to in the textual notes only when an emendation originating in some one of them is received into the text. Variants of accidentals (spelling, punctuation, capitalization) are not recorded in the notes. Contracted forms of characters' names are silently expanded in speech prefixes and stage directions, and, in the case of speech prefixes, are regularized. Additions to the stage directions of the copy-text are enclosed in brackets. Stage directions such as "within" or "aside" are enclosed in parentheses when they occur in the copy-text.

Spelling has been modernized along consciously conservative lines. "Murther" has become "murder," and "burthen," "burden," but within the limits of a modernized text, and with the following exceptions, the linguistic quality of the original has been carefully preserved. The variety of contracted forms ('em, 'am, 'm, 'um, 'hem) used in the drama of the period for the pronoun *them* are here regularly given as 'em, and the alternation between a'th' and o'th' (for *on* or *of the*) is regularly reproduced as o'th'. The copy-text distinction between preterite endings in -d and -ed is preserved except where the elision of *e* occurs in the penultimate syllable; in such cases, the final syllable is contracted. Thus, where the old editions read "threat'ned," those of the present series read "threaten'd." Where, in the old editions, a contracted preterite in -y'd would yield -i'd in modern spelling (as in "try'd," "cry'd," "deny'd"), the word is here given in its full form (e.g., "tried," "cried," "denied").

Punctuation has been brought into accord with modern practices. The effort here has been to achieve a balance between the generally light pointing of the old editions, and a system of punctuation which, without overloading the text with exclamation marks, semicolons, and dashes, will make the often loosely flowing verse (and prose) of the original syntactically intelligible to the modern reader. Dashes are regularly used only to indicate interrupted speeches, or shifts of address within a single speech.

Explanatory notes, chiefly concerned with glossing obsolete words and phrases, are printed below the textual notes at the bottom of each page. References to stage directions in the notes follow the admirable system of the Revels editions, whereby stage directions are keyed, decimally, to the line of the text before or after which they occur. Thus, a note on 0.2 has reference to the second line of the stage direction at the beginning of the scene in question. A note on 115.1 has reference to the first line of the stage direction following line 115 of the text of the relevant scene.

CYRUS HOY

University of Rochester

Contents

List of Abbreviations

Bullen	Arthur H. Bullen, ed. *The Works of Thomas Middleton.* Boston, 1885.
conj.	conjecture
cor.	corrected
Dyce	Alexander Dyce, ed. *The Works of Thomas Middleton.* London, 1840.
Dyce *seq.*	Dyce, Bullen, Sampson, and Schelling
Eccles	Mark Eccles, as quoted in Price
Maxwell	Baldwin Maxwell. "Middleton's *Michaelmas Term*," *Philological Quarterly*, XXII (1943), 29–35.
Price	George R. Price, ed. "A Critical Edition of Thomas Middleton's 'Michaelmas Term'." Unpublished dissertation, University of Wisconsin, 1941.
Q1	First Quarto of 1607
Q2	Second Quarto of 1630
Sampson	Martin W. Sampson, ed. *Thomas Middleton.* "Masterpieces of the English Drama." New York, 1915.
Schelling	Felix E. Schelling and Matthew Black, eds. *Typical Elizabethan Plays.* 3rd edn. New York, 1949.
S.D.	stage direction
S.P.	speech prefix
subs.	in substance
Sugden	Edward H. Sugden. *A Topographical Dictionary to the Works of Shakespeare and his Fellow Dramatists.* Manchester, 1925.
Tilley	Morris P. Tilley. *A Dictionary of the Proverbs in England in the Sixteenth and Seventeenth Centuries.* Ann Arbor, 1950.
uncor.	uncorrected

Introduction

I

The register of the Stationers' Company of London shows that on May 15, 1607, Arthur Johnson, the publisher,

Entered for his Copie vnder the hands of Sir Georg Buck knight & the wardens A Comedy called Mychaelmas terme[1]

and in the same year the first edition of this play appeared, a quarto with the following title page:

MICHAELMAS/ Terme./ AS/ IT HATH BEEN SVN-/ dry times acted by the Children/ *of Paules./* [ornament]/ AT LONDON,/ *Printed for A.I. and are to be/* sould at the signe of the white horse in/ Paules Churchyard./ An. 1607.

The register also records that on January 29, 1629/30, Johnson transferred his copyright in the play to Richard Meighen, who brought out the second quarto in that year:

MICHAELMAS/ TERME./ AS/ IT HATH BEENE/ SVNDRY TIMES ACTED/ BY THE CHILDREN/ of PAVLES./ *Newly corrected./* [ornament]/ *LONDON:/* Printed by *T.H.* for *R. Meighen,* and are to be sold/ at his Shop, next to the Middle-Temple Gate, and in/ S. *Dunstans* Church-yard in *Fleet-street,/* 1630.

The final notice of the play in the register is an entry of November 7, 1646, in which copyright was transferred to Meighen's widow, Mercy, and her partner Gabriel Bedell. "*Michaelmas Term,* in Quarto" is advertised as one of the "*Books Printed for, or to be sold by* M.M. G. Bedell, *and* T. Collins" in the 1654 edition of *Cabala, Mysteries of State* (Aa3ᵛ), and again in a similar list, headed "These Books are printed

[1] W. W. Greg, *A Bibliography of the English Printed Drama to the Restoration,* I (London, 1939), 22, 37, 57, 374–375; III (London, 1957), 1142–1143. Sir George Buck (or Buc) was Master of the Revels, the official licenser of plays.

for, and sold by GA. BEDELL and THO. COLLINS," in the 1656 edition of Thomas Goffe's *Three Excellent Tragedies* (R6ʳ), but this presumably was remainder stock of the 1630 quarto still on their shelves. No other edition has come down to us from this period.

There is no indication of authorship in any of these title pages or notices of the play.[2] So far as we know, *Michaelmas Term* was first assigned to Thomas Middleton in "An Exact and perfect CATALOGUE of all the PLAIES that were ever printed; together, with all the Authors names . . ." which the publisher, Edward Archer, appended to the 1656 quarto of *The Old Law* (b1ᵛ). This is a very late attribution, in a source that is far from reliable; yet it has never been seriously challenged because the play is so strikingly similar in subject matter, dramatic method, and style to the group of "city comedies" that Middleton is known to have written at this same time, most of which were also produced by the Children of St. Paul's Cathedral and published soon after that company disappeared from view in the summer of 1606.[3]

For many years attempts to fix the precise date of *Michaelmas Term* centered on the speeches in II.iii. 202–205 and 341–343, some scholars claiming that they alluded to the public execution of Francis Clarke on November 29, 1603, and others to that of Sir Everard Digby on January 30, 1605/6; but spectacles of this sort were not uncommon, and we cannot assume that Middleton had any particular one in mind. A more convincing topical allusion has since been pointed out by Baldwin Maxwell, who argued that the "sixpence British" in I.i.291 was probably one of the new coins, ordered on November 11, 1604, which designated James I as King of Great Britain (*Mag. Brit.*), the title he had assumed in that year to signify the union of England and Scotland.[4] If this is correct, it would suggest that the

---

[2] It is also listed without author in William London's *Catalogue of the Most Vendible Books in England*, published in 1658 (Greg, III, 1299; see also 1312, 1316). In "An exact and perfect Catalogue of all *Playes* that are Printed," which Richard Rogers and William Ley included in their edition of Thomas Goffe's *The Careless Shepherdess* (1656), the play is apparently assigned to "*Chapman*" (p. 5); but his name may have been crowded out of the following line (Greg, III, 1327).

[3] E. K. Chambers, *The Elizabethan Stage* (Oxford, 1923), II, 22. It is also assigned to Middleton in Francis Kirkman's catalogue (p. 10), attached to the 1661 edition of *Tom Tyler and His Wife*.

[4] Baldwin Maxwell, "Middleton's *Michaelmas Term*," *Philological Quarterly*, XXII (1943), 32.

play was written and produced sometime in 1605, after this coinage had circulated, and while it was still a matter of public interest.

Scholars have also investigated the possible sources of the play and have uncovered a number of analogues to Quomodo's scheme in some of the pamphlet exposés of London life, such as Robert Greene's *A Notable Discovery of Cozenage* (1591), which described the professional swindler or "cony-catcher."[5] Perhaps the most interesting of these is a passage in Thomas Dekker's *Lanthorn and Candelight* depicting the entrapment of a young heir by a "gull-groper" during a dice game, where we find a general parallel to Shortyard's mode of operation in II.i, and a very close one to lines 127–128 of that scene:

> The *Gull-groper* takes him to a side window and tels him, hée's sorry to sée his hard luck, but the Dice are made of womens bones, and will cozen any man, yet for his father's sake (whom he hath knowne so long) if it please him, he shall not leave off · play for a hundred pound or two.[6]

But since Dekker's work was first published in 1608, Middleton could not have borrowed from it, unless he saw it in manuscript. Indeed, he had no need to borrow from any of these pamphlets, since he could have taken his material directly from the same "source" drawn upon by the pamphleteers—the common gossip of the city. The basic stratagems used by Quomodo and his accomplices were not literary inventions but actual practices of the time, as we know from the records of contemporary trials, some of which are cited in these source studies.

It is possible that one of those trials had a special bearing upon the play which has apparently escaped notice. In his article (p. 375), R. C. Bald tentatively suggested that Quomodo himself derives from

[5] Mildred Christian, "Non-Dramatic Sources for the Rogues in Middleton's Plays" (unpublished dissertation, University of Chicago, 1932), pp. 54–59; R. C. Bald, "The Sources of Middleton's City Comedies," *Journal of English and Germanic Philology*, XXXIII (1934), 373–387; Margery Fisher, "Notes on the Sources of Some Incidents in Middleton's London Plays," *Review of English Studies*, XV (1939), 284–285; George R. Price, ed., "A Critical Edition of Thomas Middleton's 'Michaelmas Term'" (unpublished dissertation, University of Wisconsin, 1941), pp. xxii–xxviii.

[6] Ed. Oliphant Smeaton (London, 1941), p. 204; the parallel was apparently first noted by Martin W. Sampson, ed., *Thomas Middleton*, "Masterpieces of the English Drama" (New York, 1915), p. 380. See Lucetta Teagarden, "The Dekker-Middleton Problem in *Michaelmas Term*," *University of Texas Studies in English*, XXVII (1947), 49–58.

some real merchant named Howe (a pun on the meaning of the Latin word *quomodo*); and George Price followed this up, pointing out that certain lines in the play (IV.iii.11; V.iii.21) might support this hypothesis, although he was unable to find anyone of that name in his search of the membership of the Drapers', Mercers', and Goldsmiths' Companies (pp. xxix–xxx). Yet there was such a person who was convicted by the court of the Star Chamber on June 18, 1596, for a swindle similar to Quomodo's—in fact, Mildred Christian cites this case as a real-life parallel to the plot of *Michaelmas Term* (pp. 54–55), but fails to make the connection with Quomodo's name. The trial is summarized in John Hawarde's *Les Reportes del Cases in Camera Stellata, 1593–1609*, pp. 27 ff.:

The first case was an information by the Queen's Attorney against one Howe, a broker, and Easte, a solicitor, for "coseninge diuers yonge gentlemen," and procuring them to enter into bonds, statutes, recognizances and confessions of action by attorney (which bound them although under age, and which could not be avoided when they came to full age), and so of the confession of some such real action within age. They procured one Richard Cage, the only son of one John Cage of London, salter, and another . . . to swear in the Chancery, that they were of full age, in this manner: the said Howe and Easte drew a bill and an answer to it, and wrote two "councellers" names to these, without their knowledge, and procured Doctor Hone [one of the Masters of the Chancery] to write his name to the said answer; thus they condemned the gentlemen body and soul; and these "cosiners" procured money from the "erle Lincolne" for the said gentlemen, and a condition with promise of defeasance, and a confession of the action on this and other bargains, for a "perle looking glasse" of £100 and "borders" of £120, and other merchandise to the value of £600, and other "cosinages" as appears in their confession only. For which matters they were sentenced by the whole Court to have imprisonment for a year, and to be on the pillory at Westminster, at the Temple Gate, and in Cheape side, with papers on their heads, to be whipped all through the city in the four terms of the year, and fined each £20. The Lord Treasurer "would haue those y^t make the playes to make a Comedie hereof, & to acte it wth these names, & gaue good Counsell to there Fathers, y^t when they sende there

sonnes to th'innes of Cowrte to haue one or too superinten-
dentes ouer them that maye looke ouer them . . . ." [7]

Were it not for the number of years intervening, it would almost
seem that *Michaelmas Term* was Middleton's response to the Lord
Treasurer's request; in fact, he even has Quomodo point out the
social utility of this public exposure:

> for craft, once known,
> Does teach fools wit, leaves the deceiver none.
> (V.iii.90–91)

II

The portrayal of Quomodo's "craft" and its ultimate defeat is, of
course, the structural basis of the main plot of *Michaelmas Term*, and
it is primarily because of the effective development of this line of
action that the play is generally ranked, along with *A Mad World,
My Masters* and *A Trick to Catch the Old One*, as one of the most
successful of the "city comedies" which Middleton produced at the
beginning of his career.[8] All three belong to the same stage tradition—a tradition going back to Plautus and Terence, but perhaps

[7] Ed. William Baildon (London, 1894), pp. 47–48; he modernizes or
translates most of Hawarde's MS. (a mixture of English, Latin, and Law
French), but quotes certain phrases in the original spelling. An estreat
(dated July 12, 1596) of the fines imposed in Star Chamber to be levied
by the Exchequer, preserved in the memoranda rolls of the Exchequer
in the Public Record Office (E. 159/411, Trinity Term, 38 Elizabeth
[i.e., 1596], rot. 112), further identifies the defendants as Francis East,
gentleman, of Bugdon in Huntingdonshire, and William Howe, yeoman,
of Barking in Essex, and lists their fines as £40 each. I am indebted for this
information to Professor Thomas G. Barnes, who is preparing a definitive
edition of all manuscript reports of Star Chamber cases.

[8] General studies of this group of plays are to be found in Wilbur Dunkel,
The Dramatic Technique of Thomas Middleton in His Comedies of London Life
(Chicago, 1925); Una Ellis-Fermor, *The Jacobean Drama* (London, 1936),
chap. vii; L. C. Knights, *Drama and Society in the Age of Jonson* (London,
1937), chap. ix; Muriel Bradbrook, *The Growth and Structure of Elizabethan
Comedy* (London, 1955), chap. ix; Richard Barker, *Thomas Middleton* (New
York, 1958), chap. iii; Samuel Schoenbaum, "*A Chaste Maid in Cheapside*
and Middleton's City Comedy," in *Studies in the English Renaissance Drama
in Memory of Karl Julius Holzknecht*, ed. Josephine Bennett et al. (New
York, 1959), pp. 287–309; and R. B. Parker, "Middleton's Experiments
with Comedy and Judgement," in *Jacobean Theatre*, ed. John Russell
Brown and Bernard Harris (London, 1960), pp. 179–192.

best known to us in Ben Jonson's *Volpone* and *The Alchemist*—in which the action is generated by a long-range scheme of deception pitting the "wits" against the "fools," and the resultant comic effect is derived, typically, from our appreciation of the cleverness of the wits' intrigue, the discomfiture of their gullible victims, and the ironical turns through which these victims (and, often, the wits themselves) are made to contribute to their own undoing. The sequence of scenes in *Michaelmas Term* tracing the course of Quomodo's campaign against Easy very skilfully exploits the dramatic possibilities inherent in this formula; indeed, the central episode of this sequence, in II.iii, is surely Middleton's most brilliant achievement in this genre, worthy to be compared to any of the more famous "gulling" scenes in Jonson's major comedies.

Middleton's characteristic treatment of this generic formula in his city comedies is most frequently differentiated from the work of his contemporaries, and most frequently praised, in terms of its striking "realism." In *Michaelmas Term* this can be seen, for example, in the mechanics of the intrigue itself, for much of the strategy of Quomodo's master plan, from Shortyard's meeting with Easy in II.i down to the final surrender of the land in IV.i, is drawn, as was noted, from the standard repertory of the London cony-catcher—the "commodity" swindle of II.iii, upon which the whole plan turns, being one of the most notorious tricks of them all, to judge from the number of references in the literature of the day to hapless borrowers forced to accept part of their loans in over-priced and virtually unsaleable merchandise.[9]

Middleton's realism, however, is not limited to the incidents of his plot but extends to the entire dramatic world in which this plot is located. The setting of *Michaelmas Term* is the actual life of Jacobean London, vividly rendered by an accomplished satirist with a keen eye for the kind of detail that embodies and exemplifies his social milieu. For this purpose the timing of the action is particularly appropriate, since Michaelmas Term was, as the Induction explains, the chief of the four annual sessions of the law courts, when the capital was crowded with visitors coming up to engage in litigation (all major cases being tried there), or to take advantage of the

---

[9] In *Measure for Measure*, for example, we hear of a young man in debt "for a commodity of brown paper and old ginger, nine-score and seventeen pounds, of which he made five marks, ready money" (IV.iii.5–7; cf. *Michaelmas Term*, II.iii.195–197).

opportunities for pleasure or profit provided by the city's great
"season." Something of this special atmosphere is found even in the
nature of the intrigue in the main plot, which is highly legalistic
throughout, and in the incidental imagery (e.g., II.i.26–27, III.i.
46–53); but it is most fully realized in the remarkable series of genre
scenes depicting the group of country gentlemen turned "gallants,"
to which Easy belongs, in some of the typical Term diversions—
parading about the middle aisle of St. Paul's Cathedral (I.i), gambling
in a tavern (II.i), and courting a harlot (III.i). All of these scenes
contribute in some way to the two plots of this comedy, but they are
also developed in their own right to give those plots a firm grounding
in the observed life of the city.

Middleton's satirical portrait of his world, however, goes beyond
the visible surfaces of London in Term-time to record the more basic
"reality" underlying them—the economic revolution that was grad-
ually transforming a feudal society into a capitalistic one through
the transfer of wealth and power from the landed gentry to the rising
urban middle class.[10] This revolution is clearly implicated in the
very structure of the main plot, and of the subplot as well (although
in both cases the denouements reverse the historical process); in fact,
the villain-heroes of these two lines of action, Quomodo and Lethe,
can be regarded as in some sense the representatives of the new
society emerging at this time, just as their opponents, Easy, Rearage,
and Salewood, can stand (as their names suggest) for the decaying
older order. Quomodo, of course, is the ambitious "citizen" or
entrepreneur on the make, busily engaged in accumulating capital
at the expense of the gentry, and in rising up the social scale by
making his son a lawyer, marrying off his daughter to secure a
"friend at court," and, most important, acquiring a country estate
which will establish him in his new station. He is perfectly explicit
about all of this, especially in the sharply-etched domestic scene at
the beginning of II.iii, which conveys something of the intensity of
middle-class aspirations (in contrast to the picture of the prodigal
gallants in I.i, II.i, and III.i), and in the widely quoted soliloquies
where these same aspirations reappear in fantasy form (III.iv.2–18
and IV.i.64–77). And the wonderful gusto displayed in his cozening
of Easy is to be viewed, at least in part, as an expression of his acute

[10] This revolution is described in detail in Knights, *Drama and Society
in the Age of Jonson*, chaps. i–iii.

sense of the class warfare that gives an extra dimension of reality and solidity to his characterization.

Lethe, like Quomodo, is contrasted to the group of gallants (through the tensions evoked by his presence in the three scenes which focus upon them), but his "social" character is more complex and less successfully realized. Baldwin Maxwell has demonstrated that he is intended as a caricature of the Scotsmen who followed King James to London, in the early years of his reign, to make their fortunes—his true name, Andrew Gruel, being "formed from the patron saint of Scotland and the principal food of its people."[11] But he also has a more general significance; he is the "adventurer" of humble birth who, because of the social dislocations of these times, has been able to rise rapidly in the world, not by economic enterprise in the manner of Quomodo, but by the more personal route of sycophancy and influence-peddling. His assumed name implies this wider application, for while it may involve a pun on the Scotch city of Leith (as Maxwell notes), its primary reference is to the river of forgetfulness in Hades, and hence to the tendency of the social climber to deny his origins and family and former acquaintances. It suggests, as well, the more profound effects of this process upon the memory, which Lethe reveals in explaining his failure to recognize the men with whom he dined the night before:

> Oh, cry you mercy, 'tis so long ago,
> I had quite forgot you; I must be forgiven.
> Acquaintance, dear society, suits, and things
> Do so flow to me,
> That had I not the better memory,
> 'Twould be a wonder I should know myself.
>
> (I.i.166–171)[12]

Later his mistress, who is trying to rise above her station by a more

---

11 See Maxwell, "Middleton's *Michaelmas Term*," pp. 33–35, and the notes to I.i.17; II.iii.10; III.i.101, 152–162; V.iii.158.

12 Cf. I.i.266. In "The Sources of Middleton's City Comedies," p. 377, Bald says that Middleton probably derived this from Sir John Davies' thirty-first epigram, *In Priscum*; but the notion may be proverbial—see, for example, Jonson's *A Tale of a Tub*, V.iv.24, and *The Case is Altered*, V.vi.47 (ed. Herford and Simpson), Marston's *What You Will*, III.i. p. 260 (ed. Wood), and Massinger's *The Great Duke of Florence*, III.i. p. 259 (ed. Symons).

literal form of prostitution, echoes these words upon being told that her father would not know her now:

> Why, I think no less. How can he know me, when I scarce
> know myself? (III.i.30–31)

It would seem, then, that the loss of one's social roots leads to a loss of one's own identity; and this "forgetfulness" further differentiates Lethe's mode of climbing from that of Quomodo, with his strong ties to class and family, although the idea is only lightly sketched in here (it is developed much more seriously in the Dampit scenes of *A Trick to Catch the Old One*). The same must also be said of the opposition between Lethe and the gallants, which remains rather vague because no meaningful code of "manners" is established to distinguish the pretender from the true gentleman.[13] But despite these short-comings, it is clear that there is a definite attempt to place Lethe, and the type of upstart he represents, in the realistic social framework of the play.

Although all the critics have praised the realism of Middleton's backgrounds in his city comedies, some of the more discerning have pointed out that the action of these plays often borders on the fantastic. There is not so much of this in the main plot of *Michaelmas Term*, because of the nature of Quomodo's scheme, but it is evident even here in the treatment of his accomplices, Shortyard and Falselight, who suggest—with their frequent change of roles and their mis-chievous delight in them—something of the farcical tradition of the medieval "Vice."[14] And the grotesque coincidences of the subplot through which both Mother Gruel and the Country Wench's father unintentionally become the servants of their own children, without

[13] See Kathleen Lynch, *The Social Mode of Restoration Comedy* (New York, 1926), chap. ii. One has only to compare Lethe to his descendants, the Fopling Flutters and Sparkishes and Tattles of Restoration comedy, to see how important such a code can be in defining this sort of character.

[14] A similar effect is produced by the multiple disguises of Gerardine in *The Family of Love*, and Follywit in *A Mad World, My Masters*. The fact that Shortyard and Falselight are called "spirits," and the opening lines of III.iii, led Alexander Dyce to claim they were "more than mere mortal agents" (*The Works of Thomas Middleton* [London, 1840], I, 421); but later editors deny this since they have no supernatural powers, and Bald shows that "spirit" need not have this implication ("The Sources of Middleton's City Comedies," p. 380).

recognizing them, clearly belong to a different order of "reality."[15] But it is in the endings of the two plots that this shift of ground is most obvious and most objectionable. Quomodo's decision to stage his own death, which precipitates the denouement, has been compared to Volpone's similar action; but it seems less well motivated, for even though his concern for his family has been carefully established, he is given no trait equivalent to the obsessive voyeurism that drives Jonson's protagonist to this folly. Still less can be said for his sudden attack of stupidity in signing the "memorandum" in V.i, or for Shortyard's abrupt surrender to Easy earlier in this scene, or for Easy's equally abrupt acquisition of the strength and shrewdness necessary to defeat these two opponents. And in the subplot there is no real attempt to connect the various moves initiated against Lethe to his eventual arrest and exposure,[16] or to resolve the relationship between the Country Wench and her father (who simply disappears after IV.iii), or to prepare for her conversion in the final scene. Not all of the criticism that has been leveled against Middleton's conclusion is entirely justified,[17] but one can scarcely deny that it shows some signs of hasty and perfunctory workmanship.

The difficulties raised by the denouement of the main plot, moreover, involve not only this matter of probability, but also the emotional basis of the action. We are evidently expected to side with Easy and enjoy his triumph; and that is the usual response in plays belonging to this comic tradition, where the central conflict is between an improvident youth and a wealthy older man. Yet the lengthy complication has given us such a vivid impression of Quomodo's and Shortyard's brilliant mastery of the situation, and of Easy's passive gullibility, that our sympathies tend to be reversed.

[15] Lethe's encounter with Mother Gruel in I.i has been compared to the meeting of Launcelot Gobbo and his father in *The Merchant of Venice*, II.ii; and some critics have noted that the disguised parent watching over his child was a conventional stage figure (cf. Dekker's *2 Honest Whore*, Jonson's *The Staple of News*, etc., and see Northrop Frye on the "retreating paternal *eiron*"—*Anatomy of Criticism* [Princeton, 1957], pp. 174–175). This is Quomodo's role in IV.iv; but Mother Gruel (who is known to Lethe) and the Wench's father do not realize they are observing their offspring.

[16] See III.i.255–258; III.v.1–4, 57; IV.iii.43–45, 73–77.

[17] At least some of this skimping, Una Ellis-Fermor explains, "is due not so much to carelessness on the part of the author as to an understanding of the psychological condition of an audience at the end of a comedy intrigue. Once they have foreseen the end they only want it sketched, not expounded" (*The Jacobean Drama*, p. 133).

An attempt is made to rectify this at the end by insisting that Quomodo and his accomplices are justly hoist with their own petards
(V.i.41–44; V.iii.73, 164), and by rehabilitating their victim:

> But for Easy,
> Only good confidence did make him foolish,
> And not the lack of sense, that was not it;
>   (IV.iii.14–16)

but we are never wholly convinced that we should rejoice in the defeat
of those whose cleverness has been the principal source of our
pleasure, or in the victory of one of the weakest and least interesting
characters in the play.

On this point it is instructive to compare Middleton's procedure
in the other two comedies that are often grouped with *Michaelmas
Term*, since they also portray a battle of wits between the generations,
in which the crafty deceiver, ironically, brings about his own down-
fall. *A Mad World, My Masters* runs into the same problem as
Michaelmas Term, only in reverse, for young Follywit successfully
cheats his grandfather throughout the complication and then
suddenly receives his comeuppance because of a foolish blunder that,
again, violates our sense of probability and our emotional "set." In
A Trick to Catch the Old One, however, this situation is avoided by
having Lucre's cozening of his nephew, Witgood, take place before
the play begins, so that the actual representation is given over entirely
to the shrewd "trick" by which Witgood turns the tables on the
"old one," who thus becomes his "own affliction," like Quomodo,
when he is made to outsmart himself. The many admiring comments
elicited by this plot would suggest that it is the best arrangement of
the three; but if Lucre's original swindle had been depicted at
length and Witgood's retaliatory scheme relegated to the closing
scenes, we would have had the same disconcerting shift in sympathy,
and in probability, that is experienced in *Michaelmas Term*.[18]

Still another source of difficulty in this play is the relationship of
its two plots, which has received relatively little critical attention.[19]

[18] Several critics have remarked that *Michaelmas Term* could be named
A Trick to Catch the Young One, which is just another way of indicating this
difficulty (that is, if the "young one" is to engage our sympathies and win
out in the end).

[19] But see Norman Rabkin, "The Double Plot in Elizabethan Drama"
(unpublished dissertation, Harvard, 1959), pp. 208–210.

They are connected, of course, through the rivalry of Lethe and Rearage for Quomodo's daughter, Susan, but this neither affects, nor is affected by, the events of the main action in any meaningful sense—although some attempt is made to supply such a causal nexus at the beginning of II.iii (where the quarrel over these suitors seems to be one of the factors impelling Thomasine to disobey her husband and eavesdrop on the cozening scene) and, less convincingly, at the end of IV.iii and at V.iii.93–95. Their rivalry does, however, suggest a parallel to the main action, where Quomodo, Easy, and Thomasine make up another triangle which is in some ways comparable. Thus, the two men who lose out, Quomodo and Lethe, have analogous roles in their respective plots, and were also seen to occupy analogous places in the social scheme of the comedy, since they are both attempting to rise above their stations (which is why Quomodo prefers Lethe for his son-in-law); and their successful rivals, Easy and Rearage, are gentlemen. This, moreover, contributes to their success, for it explains why Thomasine urges Susan to marry Rearage and accounts, in part, for her own attraction to Easy. Her attraction has other more important sources, primarily physical, but this class distinction is certainly one of the things she has in mind when she remarks upon his superiority to Quomodo:

What difference there is in husbands, not only in one thing,
but in all. (V.i.50–51)

And it is the one thing that her daughter emphasizes, at an equivalent point in her plot, when she acknowledges Rearage's superiority to Lethe:

For now the difference appears too plain
Betwixt a base slave and a true gentleman.
(V.ii.9–10)

The immediate cause of the failure of Quomodo and Lethe to retain the affections of these women, however, is not their social status, but their involvement in another activity; it is Quomodo's scheme to get land, and his feigned death resulting from this, that first estranges Thomasine and finally frees her to marry Easy; and it is Lethe's liaison with the Country Wench that leads to his arrest and Susan's disillusionment. In fact, these activities, rather than the romantic triangles, are the real subjects of the two plots, and while the triangles establish a kind of symmetrical frame to the double-plot structure, the actual significance of that structure should depend upon some connection between the financial and the sexual preoccupations of these two components.

Such a connection is introduced in the Induction, which suggests that the primary concerns of the coming Term, and so of the play, are to be legal skulduggery (the basis of Quomodo's intrigue) and whoring; and the brief interchange between Rearage and Salewood that opens Act I links the same subjects. Throughout the dialogue, especially in the imagery, we see various equations of money and sex.[20] But the crucial connection between the two emerges out of the action of the main plot itself, where everything that Quomodo has won through his successful economic enterprise is lost through his failure in the other arena—for it is there, of course, that Thomasine finds the most compelling "difference . . . in husbands." Quomodo's inferiority to Easy in this realm is related to his age, presumably; but it also appears to be the consequence of the over-commitment of his libidinal energies to the acquisition of wealth, as evidenced, for example, in his tendency to think of the land he yearns for in sexual terms (II.iii.82–83, IV.i.110), and to regard it as an acceptable, if not preferable, substitute for a woman (I.i.99–101, V.iii.64–68). There would almost seem to be some kind of universal law in operation here, as Shortyard notes in IV.i.33–38—a law of inverse proportion regulating man's money-making and love-making abilities. And this formula involves the social dimension of the play as well, since the opposition between citizen and gentleman can also be expressed through their relationship to these two mutually exclusive categories, as it is, for instance, in the pun on Shortyard's name in I.i.88–89:

> There are too few of thy name gentlemen,
> And that we feel, but citizens in abundance;

and in Quomodo's own succinct statement of the class struggle:

> There are means and ways enow to hook in gentry,
> Besides our deadly enmity, which thus stands:
> They're busy 'bout our wives, we 'bout their lands.
>
> (I.i.105–107)

It seems appropriate, therefore, that Lethe, who is the furthest

[20] E.g., I.ii.41–44; II.i.89–91; II.iii.320–322; III.i.146–147, 257–258; III.iv.8–11, 152–156; IV.i.86–88; IV.ii.13–15.

removed from any economic base and has the highest social preten-
sions (he is trying to pass as a "courtier"), should also be the most
lecherous of all the characters. His is an extreme of excess, just as
Quomodo's is one of deficiency, and this figures in the failures of
both men in their respective triangles—Susan being alienated from
the former because she "loath[es] the sin he follows" (V.iii.117),
and her mother from the latter because "he ne'er us'd me so well as
a woman might have been us'd" (IV.iii.54–55). This entire concep-
tion is by no means unique to *Michaelmas Term*,[21] and it must be
admitted that the integration it achieves here is something less than
satisfactory, since the scenes centering upon Lethe and the Country
Wench never really come into focus in these terms—or any other,
for they remain a series of relatively discrete episodes—but it does
provide some meaningful connections between the two plots and
some coherent pattern to the play as a whole.

III

Any critical edition of *Michaelmas Term* must be based upon the
first quarto of 1607, which is the only authoritative text of the play.
Bibliographical analysis has demonstrated that it was printed in the
shops of Thomas Purfoot and Edward Allde, the former being
responsible for sheets A and B (ending at II.i.23), and the latter for
the remaining sheets, C through I.[22] Aside from the tendency to
print Middleton's verse as prose, it is a fairly accurate piece of work
by contemporary standards, with the usual number of minor misprints, and only one serious garbling of the text (V.iii.119–121).
There is no clear evidence that the manuscript behind it had been
used as a theater prompt-book; rather, the vague or inconsistent

21 A similar arrangement is found in *A Mad World, My Masters*, where,
again, the main plot is concerned with swindling and the subplot with lust,
and the successful cozener of the main plot finally comes to grief in the
sexual arena; but here too the plots are not adequately integrated. Not
until we come to the greatest of all his city comedies, *A Chaste Maid in
Cheapside*, which was written some six years later, do we find Middleton
developing these same materials of sex, money, and social class to create
a truly unified multi-plot structure.

22 See George Price, "The First Edition of *Your Five Gallants* and of
Michaelmas Term," *The Library*, 5th Series, VIII (1953), 26–29, for a
technical description of the printing of Q1 and Q2. There are, however,
many more press-corrections in Allde's section of Q1 than appear in the
copies that Price collated.

designations of some of the characters,[23] the omission of important
entrances and exits, and the "literary" cast of such stage directions
as III.i.0.1–3, IV.iv.51.1–2, and V.i.0.1, all suggest that this quarto
was set up from Middleton's own draft of the play.

The second quarto of 1630 was printed by Thomas Harper (the
"*T.H.*" of the title page) and is, despite its claim to be "*Newly
corrected*," a simple page-by-page (and, in the verse, a line-by-line)
reprint of a copy of Q1 that contained a number of uncorrected
formes. The compositor modernized the spelling and punctuation of
Q1, to a certain extent, and emended some of the misprints there;
but he also left many others unchanged and introduced new errors
of his own, some of them quite substantial (e.g., II.iii.333–335).
Since there is no reason to believe that he consulted any other text,
his corrections of Q1 possess no independent authority, and must be
judged on the same basis as the conjectures of later editors. The
press-corrections introduced during the printing of Q1 present a
more complex problem. Most of them are so obvious that they could
easily have been made, like the emendations of Q2, by an intelligent
proofreader without referring back to the original. There are, however, some others (I.i.24, 276; III.iv.215) where it seems that the
manuscript was consulted. But since we have no right to assume this
was always done,[24] a special difficulty arises in the remaining cases
(such as II.iii.344) which cannot be placed in either category with
any real assurance—cases in which the uncorrected state is not def-
initely wrong, and we cannot tell, from the nature of the emendation,
whether the proofreader checked his copy or merely relied upon his
own judgment. Fortunately, very few of the Q1 variants are of this
sort.

Michaelmas Term has been edited five times since the seventeenth
century: by Alexander Dyce (1840) and Arthur Bullen (1885) in
their editions of Middleton's collected works, by Martin Sampson
in the Middleton volume of the "Masterpieces of the English Drama"
series (1915), by Felix Schelling and Matthew Black in the second
and third editions of their anthology of Elizabethan drama (1931

[23] See the notes to the Dramatis Personae and to III.i.35.1, 36, 39;
IV.iv.27, 30, 59; and V.iii.96, 115.

[24] This proofreading took place in two separate shops, and within each
shop it was done at different times, perhaps even by different men. There
is a clear case of "mis-correction" in I.i.187, and apparently another in
III.v.71.1.

and 1949), and by George Price in an unpublished old-spelling edition (1941).[25] However, the first four of these really constitute a single "edition," for Bullen and Sampson take over Dyce's text with very little change, and the Schelling-Black text is almost a copy of Sampson's, misprints and all. Because these four are the only published versions of the play that have been available to most students, I have indicated in the notes my substantive departures from the textual tradition they have established (designated there as "Dyce *seq.*"). But these notes will show that I have much more frequently followed this tradition, since despite the inadequacy of Dyce's editorial procedure (for one thing, he seems to have worked with only a single copy of Q1, which happened to contain some uncorrected formes), he has made such an important contribution in clearing up the quarto misprints, modernizing the punctuation, supplying essential stage directions, and restoring passages of Middleton's verse which were incorrectly divided or printed as prose, that all later editors, though they may differ from him on particular details, must remain very greatly in his debt. Price's edition, the first since Dyce to be based upon a fresh examination of the quartos, has also been extremely helpful in this respect, as the textual notes will testify. For the explanatory annotation, the extensive material in Sampson and Price has proved most useful, although the briefer notes of the other editors have been drawn upon for many points.

Perhaps the most troublesome editorial problem has been that of deciding when the prose of the quartos should be read as verse. This is not easy in any case, since the well-known tendency of English speech to slip into iambic rhythms can lead one to discover lines of poetry where none were intended; and it is especially difficult in Middleton's early comedies, because the blank verse there is notoriously "loose" in structure, and often seems to be used without any artistic rationale, so that it is perfectly possible for a character to shift from verse to prose and back again within the same scene, sometimes even within the same speech. In these decisions I have generally followed the lead of Dyce or Price, as indicated in the textual notes; but I have also converted a few additional passages into verse, some without any great confidence. On this matter, it is

[25] George Price and Samuel Schoenbaum are preparing another edition of *Michaelmas Term*, to be included in a volume of Middleton's early plays which will be published as part of the "Curtain Playwrights" series by the University of Chicago Press.

not likely that any two editors will find themselves in complete agreement.

In preparing this edition, I have collated copies of Q1 in the Folger Shakespeare Library (the Clawson-Bridgewater copy), the Houghton Library at Harvard, the Henry E. Huntington Library, the Yale Elizabethan Club, and two in the British Museum (Ashley 1154, and C34.d.40), and the "Kean" copy of Q2 in the Folger; and on particular variants I have also consulted other copies of Q1 in the Folger (the Cole Orton Hall copy), the Chapin Library at Williams, the Boston Public Library, and the Carl H. Pforzheimer Library. Variants were found in the following formes of Q1: inner A, inner B, outer C, outer D, inner D (3 states), outer E (3 states), inner E, outer F (3 states), outer G (3 states), inner G, and inner I. Only the substantive variants here, and in Q2, have been recorded in the textual notes.

I wish to thank The Carl and Lily Pforzheimer Foundation, Inc., on behalf of The Carl H. Pforzheimer Library, the Trustees of the Boston Public Library, and the authorities of the other libraries and institutions cited for granting me permission to make use of this material, and the authorities of the Beinecke Rare Book and Manuscript Library at Yale for placing their Hinman collating machine at my disposal. I also would like to express my gratitude to George Price for permitting me to film his dissertation, which I have drawn upon so heavily, and to Cyrus Hoy, the general editor of the series, for patiently seeing me through this undertaking and saving me from a number of blunders, and, finally, to my wife, who bore the brunt of it all.

RICHARD LEVIN

State University of New York at Stony Brook

MICHAELMAS TERM

[DRAMATIS PERSONAE

RICHARD EASY, *a gentleman of Essex*
REARAGE ⎫
SALEWOOD ⎬ *London gallants*
COCKSTONE ⎭
EPHESTIAN QUOMODO, *a woolen draper*   5
SIM, *his son*
SHORTYARD, *alias* JOHN BLASTFIELD, *etc.* ⎫
FALSELIGHT, *alias* IDEM, *etc.*   ⎬ *Quomodo's accomplices*
ANDREW LETHE, *born* ANDREW GRUEL, *an upstart adventurer*
DICK HELLGILL, *Lethe's pander*   10
COUNTRY WENCH'S FATHER
DUSTBOX, *a scrivener*
BOY, *Quomodo's servant*
THOMASINE, *Quomodo's wife*
SUSAN, *their daughter*   15
COUNTRY WENCH, *Lethe's mistress*
MOTHER GRUEL, *Lethe's mother*
MOTHER, *an older woman, friend of Thomasine*
WINIFRED, *Thomasine's maid*
MISTRESS COMINGS, *a tirewoman*   20
JUDGE, TAILOR, DRAWER, OFFICERS, MOURNERS, SERVANTS, *etc.*

MICHAELMAS TERM ⎫
BOY, *his servant*   ⎬ *In the Induction*
HILARY TERM, EASTER TERM, TRINITY TERM
POOR FELLOW, PAGE, PANDER, *in the dumb show* ⎭   25

The scene: *London*]

DRAMATIS PERSONAE] *Dyce*
(*subs.*); *not in Q 1–2.*

2–3. *Rearage, Salewood*] The names suggest spendthrifts who are in debt
("arrears") and have sold their ancestral estates.

5. *woolen draper*] cloth merchant.

7–8. *Shortyard, Falselight*] Dishonest merchants used inaccurate measuring
rods and kept their shops dimly lit to cheat customers.

9. *Andrew Lethe, Gruel*] On the significance of his names, see Introduction,
p. xvi.

10. *Hellgill*] Pander in some S.P.s and S.D.s.

12. *scrivener*] public scribe and notary, who carried a "dustbox" filled
with sand to blot ink.

14. *Thomasine*] feminine, and diminutive, form of "Thomas."

16. *Country Wench*] Courtesan in S.P.s after I.ii, and *Courtesan* or *Harlot*
in S.D.s after III.i.

20. *tirewoman*] hairdresser; her name puns on "combings" (Price).

Michaelmas Term

INDUCTIO

Enter Michaelmas Term *in a whitish cloak, new come up out of the country,
a* Boy *bringing his gown after him.*

MICHAELMAS TERM.

    Boy!

BOY.   Here, sir.

MICHAELMAS TERM.   Lay by my conscience,

    Give me my gown, that weed is for the country;

    We must be civil now, and match our evil;

    Who first made civil black, he pleas'd the devil.

    So, now know I where I am, methinks already   5

    I grasp best part of the autumnian blessing

    In my contentious fathom; my hand's free,

    From wronger and from wronged I have fee,

    And what by sweat from the rough earth they draw

    Is to enrich this silver harvest, Law;   10

    And so through wealthy variance and fat brawl,

    The barn is made but steward to the hall.

    Come they up thick enough?

BOY.

    Oh, like hops and harlots, sir.

MICHAELMAS TERM.

    Why dost thou couple them?   15

1–2. Lay . . . gown] *Dyce; one line
in Q 1–2.*

---

2. *weed*] his cloak; its whiteness represents his "country conscience"
(Price).

3. *civil*] citified.

4. *civil black*] Civic and guild officials, lawyers, etc., often wore gowns of
black, which was the devil's color.

6. *autumnian*] Michaelmas Term began on October 9.

7. *fathom*] embrace, power.

12. *hall*] law court, i.e., "crops finance law-suits" (Price).

13. *Come they up*] litigants coming to London for the Term.

BOY.

> Oh, very aptly, for as the hop well boiled will make a man
> not stand upon his legs, so the harlot in time will leave a
> man no legs to stand upon.

MICHAELMAS TERM.

> Such another, and be my heir! I have no child,
> Yet have I wealth would redeem beggary.   20
> I think it be a curse both here and foreign,
> Where bags are fruitful'st, there the womb's most barren;
> The poor has all our children, we their wealth.
> Shall I be prodigal when my life cools,
> Make those my heirs whom I have beggar'd, fools?   25
> It would be wondrous; rather beggar more;
> Thou shalt have heirs enow, thou keep'st a whore.
> And here comes kindred too with no mean purses,
> Yet strive to be still blest with clients' curses.

Music playing. Enter the other three Terms, *the first bringing in a fellow
poor, which the other two advanceth, giving him rich apparel, a page, and a
pander.*   *Exit* [*fellow*].

MICHAELMAS TERM.

> What subtlety have we here? A fellow   30
> Shrugging for life's kind benefits, shift and heat,
> Crept up in three Terms, wrapt in silk and silver,
> So well appointed too with page and pander;
> It was a happy gale that blew him hither.

34. hither] *Q2;* hether *Q1.*

---

16. *hop well boiled*] in malt liquors.

18. *no legs*] because of venereal disease.

19. *Such another*] another remark as clever as that.

22. *bags*] moneybags.   24. *cools*] draws to an end.

27. *Thou*] himself, according to previous editors; but l. 19 would suggest
that he is still addressing the Boy.

27. *enow*] enough.

29.1. *three Terms*] Hilary (winter), Easter (early spring), and Trinity
(late spring). Michaelmas is the *father* (l. 35) since it was the first Term of
the legal year (Sampson).

29.1. *fellow*] Price notes the similarity between his career and Lethe's.

31. *Shrugging*] shivering.

31. *shift*] clothing.   33. *appointed*] equipped.

34. *gale . . . hither*] proverbial (Tilley, W 441). Q1 *hether* is an earlier
form of *hither* (cf. III.i.268, V.iii.158; see also IV.i.50, V.i.93).

FIRST TERM.

    Thou father of the Terms, hail to thee.   35

SECOND TERM.

    May much contention still keep with thee.

THIRD TERM.

    Many new fools come up and fee thee.

SECOND TERM.

    Let 'em pay dear enough that see thee.

FIRST TERM.

    And like asses use such men;

    When their load's off, turn 'em to graze again.   40

SECOND TERM.

    And may our wish have full effect,

    Many a suit, and much neglect.

THIRD TERM.

    And as it hath been often found,

    Let the clients' cups come round.

SECOND TERM.

    Help your poor kinsmen, when you ha' got 'em;   45

    You may drink deep, leave us the bottom.

THIRD TERM.

    Or when there is a lamb fall'n in,

    Take you the lamb, leave us the skin.

MICHAELMAS TERM.

    Your duty and regard hath mov'd us,

    Never till now we thought you lov'd us;   50

    Take comfort from our words, and make no doubt

    You shall have suits come sixteen times about.

ALL THREE TERMS.

    We humbly thank the patron of our hopes.   *Exeunt.*

MICHAELMAS TERM.

    With what a vassal-appetite they gnaw

    On our reversions, and are proud   55

    Coldly to taste our meats, which eight returns

    Serve in to us as courses.

---

45. *'em*] clients' cups (wealth).   47. *lamb*] victim (a client).

48. *skin*] to make parchment for legal documents.

55. *reversions*] leftovers.

56. *returns*] days on which writs and mandates had to be returned to court; there were eight in Michaelmas Term (Sampson).

One day our writs, like wild-fowl, fly abroad,
And then return o'er cities, towns, and hills,
With clients, like dried straws, between their bills;   60
And 'tis no few, birds pick to b d their nests,
Nor no small money that keeps drabs and feasts!
But, gentlemen, to spread myself open unto you, in cheaper
Terms I salute you; for ours have but sixpenny fees all the
year long, yet we dispatch you in two hours, without demur; 65
your suits hang not long here after candles be lighted. Why
call we this play by such a dear and chargeable title, *Michaelmas Term*? Know it consents happily to our purpose, though
perhaps faintly to the interpretation of many, for he that
expects any great quarrels in law to be handled here will be 70
fondly deceived; this only presents those familiar accidents
which happen'd in town in the circumference of those six
weeks whereof Michaelmas Term is lord. *Sat sapienti*; I
hope there's no fools i'th' .   *Exit* [*with* Boy].

---

67. call we] *this edn.;* we call *Q 1–*   *7*4. S.D. *Exit*] *Q 1; not in Q 2.
Dyce seq.*

---

61. *few*] *straws* (l. 60) understood Price).
61. *nests*] The quarto spelling, *neasts*, indicates the rhyme.
62. *drabs*] prostitutes.
64. *ours*] the actors' (the Children of St. Paul's).
65. *two hours*] Plays at St. Paul's did not begin before four, after prayers, and the gates shut at six (E. K. Chambers, *The Elizabethan Stage* [Oxford, 1923], II, 21).
65. *demur*] delay (Price).
66. *hang*] linger.
67. *call we*] Dyce *seq.* retain *we call*, and then must alter *Term? Know* (l. 68) to *Term, know* to form a declarative sentence (ending l. 73). But it seems more likely that the sentence break at l. 68 is correct, and that the compositor mistakenly transposed *call we* (or perhaps dropped *do* after *Why*).
67. *dear and chargeable*] costly, burdensome.
68. *consents*] agrees, fits in.
68. *happily*] felicitously, fortunately.
71. *fondly*] foolishly.
72. *circumference*] space.
73. *Sat sapienti*] shortened form of the proverbial expression found in Plautus' *Persa* (l. 729) and Terence's *Phormio* (l. 541): *dictum sapienti sat est*—"a word to the wise is sufficient."

[I.i] *Enter at one door* Master Rearage, *meeting* Master Salewood.

SALEWOOD.

What, Master Rearage?

REARAGE.

Master Salewood? Exceedingly well met in town. Comes
your father up this Term?

SALEWOOD.

Why, he was here three days before the Exchequer gap'd.

REARAGE.

Fie, such an early Termer?   5

SALEWOOD.

He's not to be spoke withal; I dare not ask him blessing,
till the last of November.

REARAGE.

And how looks thy little venturing cousin?

SALEWOOD.

Faith, like a lute that has a   strings broke, nobody will
meddle with her.   10

REARAGE.

Fie, there are doctors enow own will string her again,
and make her sound as swee as e'er she did. Is she not
married yet?

SALEWOOD.

Sh'as no luck; some may better steal a horse than others
look on. I have known a virgin of five bastards wedded. 15
Faith, when all's done we must be fain to marry her into the
North, I'm afraid.

REARAGE.

But will she pass so, think you?

SALEWOOD.

Puh, any thing that is warm enough is good enough for

I.i] *Dyce; no scene division in Q1–2.*   0.1. *meeting*] *Q2; meetiug Q1.*

---

4. *Exchequer*] court dealing with state revenues, which opened (*gap'd*)
eight days before Michaelmas Term (Price).

7. *November*] Michaelmas Term ended on November 28.

8. *venturing*] venturesome.

14–15. *some . . . on*] proverbial (Tilley, H 692).

16. *fain*] obliged.

17. *North*] probably Scotland (Maxwell); cf. V.iii.122–123.

them; so it come in the likeness, though the devil be in't,   20
they'll venture the firing.

REARAGE.

They're worthy spirits, i'faith. Heard you the news?

SALEWOOD.

Not yet.

REARAGE.

Mistress Difficult is newly fall'n a widow.

SALEWOOD.

Say true, is Master Difficult, the lawyer, dead?   25

REARAGE.

Easily dead, sir.

SALEWOOD.

Pray, when died he?

REARAGE.

What a question's that! When should a lawyer die but in the
vacation? He has no leisure to die in the Term-time; beside,
the noise there would fetch him again.   30

SALEWOOD.

Knew you the nature of his disease?

REARAGE.

Faith, some say he died of an old grief he had, that the
vacation was fourteen weeks long.

SALEWOOD.

And very likely; I knew 'twould kill him at last, 't'as
troubled him a long time. He was one of those that would   35
fain have brought in the heresy of a fifth Term, often crying,
with a loud voice, "Oh, why should we lose Barthol'mew
week?"

24. newly] *Q1 (cor.); not in Q1
(uncor.), Q2.*

---

21. *venture the firing*] take the risk (Schelling).

24. *newly*] Evidently the proofreader consulted the MS. here. (Middleton
uses the identical phrase in *A Trick to Catch the Old One*, IV.iv.215–216.)

29. *vacation*] preceding Michaelmas Term (Sampson).

30. *fetch him*] back from the dead.

36. *fain*] gladly.

37–38. *Barthol'mew week*] week of the great London fair (St. Bartholomew's Day was August 24).

REARAGE.

He savors, stop your nose; no more of him.

Enter Master Cockstone, *a gentleman, meeting* Master Easy *of Essex.*

COCKSTONE.

Young Master Easy, let me salute you, sir. When came you? 40

EASY.

I have but inn'd my horse since, Master Cockstone.

COCKSTONE.

You seldom visit London, Master Easy,
But now your father's dead, 'tis your only course;
Here's gallants of all sizes, of all lasts;
Here you may fit your foot, make choice of those 45
Whom your affection may rejoice in.

EASY.

You have easily possess'd me, I am free;
Let those live hinds that know not liberty.

COCKSTONE.

Master Rearage?

EASY.

Good Master Salewood, I am proud of your society. 50

REARAGE.

What gentleman might that be?

COCKSTONE.

One Master Easy; h'as good land in Essex,
A fair free-breasted gentleman, somewhat too open
(Bad in man, worse in woman,
The gentry-fault at first); he is yet fresh, 55
And wants the city powd'ring. But what news?
Is't yet a match 'twixt Master Quomodo's
The rich draper's daughter and yourself?

57–58.] *Dyce; prose in Q 1–2.*

---

39. *savors*] smells.   41. *inn'd*] lodged in the stable of an inn.
41. *since*] since arriving in town.
47. *possess'd*] persuaded (Dyce).   48. *hinds*] country boors.
52. *Essex*] rural county northeast of London; its people were "typed"
rustic simpletons (Sudgen).
55. *gentry . . . first*] typical weakness of the gentry.
56. *wants*] lacks, needs.   56. *powd'ring*] seasoning.

REARAGE.

    Faith, sir, I am vildly rival'd.

COCKSTONE.

    Vildly? By whom?   60

REARAGE.

    One Andrew Lethe, crept to a little warmth,
    And now so proud that he forgets all storms;
    One that ne'er wore apparel but, like ditches,
    'Twas cast before he had it, now shines bright
    In rich embroideries. Him Master Quomodo affects,   65
    The daughter him, the mother only me;
    I rest most doubtful, my side being weakest.

COCKSTONE.

    Yet the mother's side
    Being surer than the father's, it may prove,
    "Men plead for money best, women for love."   70

REARAGE.

    'Slid, Master Quomodo!

COCKSTONE.

    How then, afraid of a woolen draper?

REARAGE.

    He warn'd me his house, and I hate he should see me abroad.

                                [They all retire.]

    [Enter] Quomodo *with his two spirits,* Shortyard *and* Falselight.

QUOMODO.

    Oh my two spirits, Shortyard and Falselight, you that have

61–67.] *Dyce; prose in* Q *1–2.*   73.1.] *Dyce.*

---

    59. *vildly*] vilely.   61. *warmth*] comfort, security.

    64. *cast*] meant both to clear out (*ditches*) and to discard or cast off (*apparel*).

    65. *affects*] likes, favors, aims at.

    66. *mother only me*] only the mother (affects) me.

    69. *surer*] "more certain regarding parentage" (Sampson).

    70.] In Q1–2 the line begins with the initial quotation marks (or "gnomic pointing") used to set off aphoristic sentences.

    71. *'Slid*] common oath, "God's lid."

    73. *warn'd me*] ordered me away from.

    73.1. *retire*] move off to another part of the stage (probably the rear), but do not exit.

    73.2. *spirits*] see Introduction, p. xvii.

so enrich'd me. I have industry for you both!   75

SHORTYARD.

Then do you please us best, sir.

QUOMODO.

Wealthy employment.

SHORTYARD.

You make me itch, sir.

QUOMODO.

You, Falselight, as I have directed you—

FALSELIGHT.

I am nimble.   80

QUOMODO.

Go, make my coarse commodities look sleek,
With subtle art beguile the honest eye;
Be near to my trap-window, cunning Falselight.

FALSELIGHT.

I never fail'd it yet.   *Exit* Falselight.

QUOMODO.   I know thou didst not.—
But now to thee, my true and secret Shortyard,   85
Whom I dare trust e'en with my wife;
Thou ne'er didst mistress harm, but master good;
There are too few of thy name gentlemen,
And that we feel, but citizens in abundance.
I have a task for thee, my pregnant spirit,   90
To exercise thy pointed wits upon.

---

78. itch] *Q2;* icth *Q1.*   81–83.] *Dyce; prose in Q1–2.*
81. commodities look sleek] *Q2;*   89. in] *Sampson; not in Q1–2.*
commodities, looke, seeke *Q1.*

---

75. *industry*] occupation (Sampson).

81–83.] see Dramatis Personae, ll. 7–8, note.

83. *trap-window*] hinged window or movable penthouse that was lowered
to dim the light (Sampson, who cites Middleton and Rowley's *The World
Tossed at Tennis*, l. 455: "false lights, cozening trap-windows").

85–89.] *double-entendre,* since *yard* (measuring rod) was a slang term for
the penis.

89. *citizens*] men admitted to the "freedom" of the city (I.ii.44) through
membership in a guild, i.e., tradesmen as opposed to gentlemen (cf. l. 132).

89. *in*] Price believes "of" is understood before *citizens;* but Sampson's
insertion (perhaps an oversight, since it is not annotated) yields a clearer
and more natural construction and preserves the parallelism.

90. *pregnant*] resourceful, quick-witted.

SHORTYARD.

 Give it me, for I thirst.

QUOMODO.   Thine ear shall drink it.

 Know, then, I have not spent this long vacation

 Only for pleasure's sake. Give me the man

 Who out of recreation culls advantage,   95

 Dives into seasons, never walks but thinks,

 Ne rides but plots. My journey was toward Essex—

SHORTYARD.

 Most true.

QUOMODO. Where I have seen what I desire.

SHORTYARD.

 A woman?

QUOMODO. Puh, a woman! Yet beneath her,

 That which she often treads on, yet commands her: 100

 Land, fair neat land.

SHORTYARD.   What is the mark you shoot at?

QUOMODO.

 Why, the fairest to cleave the heir in twain,

 I mean his title; to murder his estate,

 Stifle his right in some detested prison.

 There are means and ways enow to hook in gentry, 105

 Besides our deadly enmity, which thus stands:

 They're busy 'bout our wives, we 'bout their lands.

SHORTYARD.

 Your revenge is more glorious:

 To be a cuckold is but for one life,

 When land remains to you, your heir, or wife. 110

QUOMODO.

 Ah, sirrah, do we sting 'em? This fresh gallant

99–107. Puh . . . lands] *Dyce; prose* 104. some] *Q2;* some some *Q1.*
in Q1–2.   111–112. Ah . . . me] *Dyce; prose in*
102. heir] *Q1;* haire *Q2.*   *Q1–2.*

 93. *long vacation*] see ll. 32–38.

 96. *Dives into seasons*] probes into occasions, seizes opportunities.

 97. *Ne*] nor; but perhaps a misprint for "Ne'er" (Eccles).

 101. *neat*] trim, handsome (Eccles).

 102. *heir*] punning on "hair" (see textual note). The imagery (*mark, shoot, cleave*) is drawn from archery.

 103. *title*] to his lands.

 104. *prison*] for debtors (see II.iii.345, note).

Rode newly up before me.

SHORTYARD.   I beseech his name.

QUOMODO.

Young Master Easy.

SHORTYARD.   Easy? It may fall right.

QUOMODO.

I have inquir'd his haunt. —Stay, hah!

Ay, that! 'Tis, that's he, that's he!   115

SHORTYARD.

Happily!

QUOMODO.

Observe, take surely note of him, he's fresh and free;

Shift thyself speedily into the shape of gallantry;

I'll swell thy purse with angels.

Keep foot by foot with him, out-dare his expenses,   120

Flatter, dice, and brothel to him;

Give him a sweet taste of sensuality;

Train him to every wasteful sin, that he

May quickly need health, but especially money;

Ravish him with a dame or two, be his bawd for once,   125

I'll be thine forever;

Drink drunk with him, creep into bed to him,

Kiss him and undo him, my sweet spirit.

SHORTYARD.

Let your care dwell in me, soon shall it shine;

What subtlety is in man, that is not mine?   *Exit.* 130

QUOMODO.

Oh, my most cheerful spirit, go, dispatch!

Gentry is the chief fish we tradesmen catch.   *Exit.*

EASY.

What's here?

114–128.] *Price (subs.); prose in*   115. that! 'Tis] *this edn.;* that, 'tis
Q 1–2.   *Q 1–2;* that 'tis *Dyce seq.*

---

114. *haunt*] where he lodges.

118. *shape of gallantry*] dress of a gallant.

119. *angels*] gold coins worth about ten shillings.

123. *Train*] draw, entice.

127. *bed*] Elizabethan men slept together as a habit of friendliness (Sampson); see II.iii.156.

SALEWOOD.

    Oh, they are bills for chambers.

EASY [*reading bill*].

    "Against Saint Andrew's, at a painter's house, there's a fair 135
    chamber ready furnish'd to be let, the house not only endued
    with a new fashion forepart, but, which is more convenient
    for a gentleman, with a very provident back door."

SALEWOOD.

    Why, here's virtue still; I like that thing that's necessary
    as well as pleasant.   140

        [*Enter* Lethe, *studying the bills.*]

COCKSTONE.

    What news in yonder paper?

REARAGE.   Hah! Seek you

    For news? There's for you!

SALEWOOD.   Who? 'Tis!

    In the name of the black angels, Andrew Gruel!

REARAGE.

    No, Andrew Lethe.

SALEWOOD.   Lethe?

REARAGE.   H'as forgot

    His father's name, poor Walter Gruel, that begot   145

140.1.] *Price* (*subs.*), *relocating Dyce.*   142. Who? 'Tis!] *Price conj.;* Whose
141–147.] *Price* (*subs.*), *revising Dyce;*   tis? *Q1;* Who's this? *Q2, Dyce seq.*
prose in Q1–2.

---

    134. *bills*] advertisements. The scene is located in the middle aisle of
St. Paul's Cathedral, a popular gathering place where notices of this type
were posted (Dyce).

    135. *Against*] near or facing this church (Sugden).

    137. *forepart*] front.

    138. *back door*] to avoid his creditors or, as Sampson suggests, to escape
if surprised in a romantic intrigue.

    139. *necessary*] needful, useful.

    142. *Who? 'Tis!*] Price's conjecture that the compositor misread MS.
? as terminal "s" seems most convincing (cf. V.i.100). See l. 115 for a
similar use of '*Tis* as an independent clause (eliminated in Dyce *seq.*), and
IV.iv.54.

    143. *black angels*] devils (see Induction, l. 4, note).

    145. *Walter*] pronounced "water" (Price), cheapening the *gruel*. Cf. the
mercer, Wa(l)ter Chamlet (watered camlet, a fabric), in Middleton and
Webster's *Anything for a Quiet Life.*

Him, fed him, and brought him up.

SALEWOOD.   Not hither?

REARAGE.   No,
'Twas from his thoughts; he brought him up below.

SALEWOOD.

But does he pass for Lethe?

REARAGE.   'Mongst strange eyes
That no more know him than he knows himself,
That's nothing now, for Master Andrew Lethe,   150
A gentleman of most received parts,
Forgetfulness, lust, impudence, and falsehood,
And one especial courtly quality,
To wit, no wit at all. I am his rival
For Quomodo's daughter, but he knows it not.   155

SALEWOOD.

H'as spied us o'er his paper.

REARAGE.   Oh, that's a warning
To make our duties ready.

COCKSTONE.   Salute him? Hang him!

REARAGE.

Puh, wish his health awhile, he'll be laid shortly;
Let him gorge venison for a time, our doctors
Will bring him to dry mutton. Seem respective,   160
To make his pride swell like a toad with dew.

SALEWOOD.

Master Lethe!

REARAGE.

Sweet Master Lethe!

LETHE.

Gentlemen, your pardon; I remember you not.

SALEWOOD.

Why, we sup'd with you last night, sir!   165

149–161.] *Dyce; prose in Q 1–2.*

---

147. *below*] in an inferior status (cf. ll. 280–281).
148. *strange*] strangers'.   151. *received parts*] recognized talents.
157. *duties*] dutiful salutations.   158. *laid*] laid low, prostrated.
160. *dry mutton*] prescribed diet in treating syphilis (cf. Middleton's
Your Five Gallants, I.i.324–329).
160. *respective*] respectful (Dyce).
161. *swell . . . toad*] proverbial (Tilley, T 362).

LETHE.

> Oh, cry you mercy, 'tis so long ago,
> I had quite forgot you; I must be forgiven.
> Acquaintance, dear society, suits, and things
> Do so flow to me,
> That had I not the better memory,   170
> 'Twould be a wonder I should know myself.
> "Esteem is made of such a dizzy metal."
> I have receiv'd of many, gifts o'er night
> Whom I have forgot ere morning; meeting the men,
> I wish'd 'em to remember me again;   175
> They do so, then if I forget again,
> I know what help'd before, that will help then.
> This is my course, for memory I have been told
> Twenty preserves, the best I find is gold.
> Ay, truly! Are you not knights yet, gentlemen?   180

SALEWOOD.

> Not yet.

LETHE.

> No? That must be look'd into, 'tis your own fault. I have
> some store of venison; where shall we devour it, gentlemen?

SALEWOOD.

> The Horn were a fit place.

LETHE.

> For venison fit,   185
> The horn having chas'd it,
> At the Horn we'll—

169–170.] *Dyce; one line in Q1–2.*   horne weele—Rime *Q1* (*uncor.*),
187–188.] *Dyce; one line in Q1–2;*   *Q2;* horne—weele Rime *Q1* (*cor.*).

---

168. *dear*] choice (Price).   168. *suits*] petitions.
172. *Esteem*] popularity (Sampson) or prestige. This line is set off by
gnomic pointing (see l. 70, note).
172. *dizzy metal*] dizzying substance (Price).   175. *wish'd*] asked.
175. *remember me*] remind me (with another gift).
179. *preserves*] preservatives (Sampson).
180. *Are...yet*] a thrust at the large number of knights created by
James I.
184. *The Horn*] popular tavern on Fleet Street (Sugden).
186. *horn*] of the hunters in the deer *park* (l. 192).
187–188.] The press correction is clearly wrong, since the supplied
rhymes require *we'll.*

Rhyme to that?

COCKSTONE.

Taste it.

SALEWOOD. Waste it.

REARAGE.   Cast it.

LETHE.

That's the true rhyme, indeed.   190

We hunt our venison twice, I tell you,

First out o'th' park, next out o'th' belly.

COCKSTONE.

First dogs take pains to make it fit for men,

Then men take pain to make it fit for dogs.

LETHE.

Right.   195

COCKSTONE.

Why, this is kindness; a kind gallant, you,

And love to give the dogs more than their due.

We shall attend you, sir.

LETHE.   I pray do so.

SALEWOOD.

The Horn.

LETHE.   Easily remember'd that, you know!

Exeunt [all but Lethe].

But now unto my present business. The daughter yields, and 200
Quomodo consents, only my Mistress Quomodo, her mother,
without regard runs full against me, and sticks hard. Is
there no law for a woman that will run upon a man at her
own apperil? Why should not she consent, knowing my state,
my sudden fortunes? I can command a custard, and other 205
bake-meats, death of sturgeon; I could keep house with

190–192.] *this edn.; prose in Q1–2.*   196. is] *Q1 (cor.); not in Q1 (uncor.),*
194. pain] *Q1;* paines *Q2, Dyce seq.*   *Q2.*

---

189. *Cast*] vomit (Bullen).   193. *dogs*] in the hunt.
194. *pain*] This seems more idiomatic than the Q2 reading adopted by
Dyce *seq.*, and emphasizes the word-play.
194. *fit for dogs*] who eat vomit.
202. *runs full against*] absolutely opposes.   202. *sticks*] persists.
204. *apperil*] peril (Dyce).   205. *command*] get for the asking.
206. *death of sturgeon*] perhaps an oath (Bullen), or a keg of sturgeon
(Sampson); the text may be corrupt.

nothing. What friends have I! How well am I beloved, e'en
quite throughout the scullery! Not consent? 'Tis e'en as I
have writ; I'll be hang'd and she love me not herself, and
would rather preserve me as a private friend to her own 210
pleasures, than any way advance her daughter upon me to
beguile herself. Then how have I relieved her in that point?
Let me peruse this letter.

[*Reading.*] "Good Mistress Quomodo, or rather, as I
hope ere the Term end, Mother Quomodo, since only your 215
consent keeps aloof off, and hinders the copulation of your
daughter, what may I think, but that it is a mere affection in
you, doting upon some small inferior virtue of mine, to draw
me in upon yourself? If the case stand so, I have comfort
for you; for this you may well assure yourself, that by the 220
marriage of your daughter I have the better means and
opportunity to yourself, and without the least suspicion."

This is moving stuff, and that works best with a citizen's
wife. But who shall I get to convey this now? My page I ha'
lent forth; my pander I have employ'd about the country to 225
look out some third sister, or entice some discontented
gentlewoman from her husband, whom the laying out of my
appetite shall maintain. Nay, I'll deal like an honorable
gentleman, I'll be kind to women; that which I gather i'th'
day, I'll put into their purses at night. You shall have no 230
cause to rail at me; no, faith, I'll keep you in good fashion,
ladies; no meaner men than knights shall ransom home your
gowns and recover your smocks; I'll not dally with you.

---

208. *scullery*] kitchen, presumably at Court (Eccles).

209. *and she*] if she.

216. *keeps aloof off*] remains withheld.

217. *mere*] sheer (Price).

226. *look out*] look out for, seek out.

226. *third sister*] Since daughters were often married off by seniority, a
girl with two older unwed sisters might well despair of ever marrying
(especially if, as Price suggests, the family cannot afford three dowries),
and so be susceptible.

227. *laying out*] exercising, expenditure.

230–233. *You . . . you*] addressed to the audience (Price). Cf. Middleton's
A Mad World, My Masters, IV.v.20: "by your favor, ladies."

232. *ransom home*] from pawn (Sampson).

233. *smocks*] women's undergarments.

Some poor widow woman would come as a necessary
bawd now; and see where fitly comes—   235

[*Enter* Mother Gruel.]

My mother! Curse of poverty! Does she come up to shame
me, to betray my birth, and cast soil upon my new suit?
Let her pass me, I'll take no notice of her. Scurvy murrey
kersey!

MOTHER GRUEL.

By your leave, and like your worship—   240

LETHE [*aside*].

Then I must proudly venture it. —To me, good woman?

MOTHER GRUEL.

I beseech one word with your worship.

LETHE.

Prithee, be brief then.

MOTHER GRUEL.

Pray, can your worship tell me any tidings of one Andrew
Gruel, a poor son of mine own?   245

LETHE.

I know a gallant gentleman of the name, one Master Andrew
Gruel, and well receiv'd amongst ladies.

MOTHER GRUEL.

That's not he, then. He is no gentleman that I mean.

LETHE.

Good woman, if he be a Gruel, he's a gentleman i'th'
mornings, that's a gentleman o'th' first; you cannot tell me. 250

MOTHER GRUEL.

No, truly, his father was an honest upright tooth-drawer.

235.1.] *Dyce.*   243. Prithee] *Q1* (Prethe); Preth
236. of] *Q2;* off *Q1.*   *Q2.*
241. S.D.] *Sampson.*   248. That's . . . then] *Dyce; separate
                                     line in Q1–2.*

---

237. *cast soil*] besmirch, stain.
238–239. *murrey kersey*] mulberry-colored coarse cloth.
240. *and*] if it.
249–250. *if . . . mornings*] since gentlemen ate gruel for breakfast (Price).
250. *o'th' first*] first rank (Price) or truest, since breakfast began the day
(cf. *A Mad World, My Masters,* I.i.83: "Here's a mad-brain o'th' first").
251. *tooth-drawer*] dentist, regarded as a very low occupation; pro-
verbially, a very thin and meager fellow (Tilley, T 434).

LETHE.

Oh, my teeth!

MOTHER GRUEL.

An't please your worship, I have made a sore journey on't,
all this vacant time, to come up and see my son Andrew.
Poor Walter Gruel, his father, has laid his life, and left me a 255
lone woman; I have not one husband in all the world. Therefore my coming up is for relief, an't like your worship, hoping
that my son Andrew is in some place about the kitchen—

LETHE.

Kitchen! Puh, fah!

MOTHER GRUEL.

Or a servingman to some knight of worship.   260

LETHE [aside].

Oh, let me not endure her! —Know you not me, good
woman?

MOTHER GRUEL.

Alas, an't please your worship, I never saw such a glorious
suit since the hour I was kersen'd.

LETHE [aside].

Good, she knows me not, my glory does disguise me;   265
Beside, my poorer name being drench'd in Lethe,
She'll hardly understand me. What a fresh air can do!
I may employ her as a private drudge
To pass my letters and secure my lust,

---

253. on't] *Price conj.;* out *Q 1–2,*   261. S.D.] *Dyce.*
Dyce seq.   265. S.D.] *Dyce.*
260. knight] *Q 2;* Kinght *Q 1.*   265. disguise] *Dyce;* disquire *Q 1–2.*

---

253. *An't*] if it.

253. *on't*] Going to London would not be a journey *out* (see textual note);
if any adverb followed, it would be "up" (cf. Induction, ll. 0.1, 13; I.i.112,
254, 257; II.i.66, etc.). The compositor may have misread the MS., or
reversed the "n" in his type (cf. II.ii.33, III.iv.229, IV.ii.28).

254. *vacant time*] vacation (Sampson).

255. *laid his life*] died.   258. *place*] of employment, job.

264. *kersen'd*] christened.   265. *glory*] glorious clothing.

266. *poorer name*] Gruel.

266. *drench'd in Lethe*] obliterated by my new name; and forgotten by
being dipped in the river of oblivion.

267. *understand*] recognize (Price).

267. *air*] appearance, bearing.   269. *pass*] deliver.

And ne'er be noted mine, to shame my blood,   270
And drop my staining birth upon my raiment.—
Faith, good woman, you will hardly get to the speech of
Master Andrew, I tell you.

MOTHER GRUEL.

No? Marry, hang him, and like your worship, I have known
the day when nobody car'd to speak to him.   275

LETHE.

You must take heed how you speak ill of him now, I can tell
you; he's so employ'd.

MOTHER GRUEL.

Employ'd for what?

LETHE.

For his behavior, wisdom, and other virtues.

MOTHER GRUEL.

His virtues? No, 'tis well known his father was too poor a 280
man to bring him up to any virtues; he can scarce write and
read.

LETHE.

He's the better regarded for that amongst courtiers, for
that's but a needy quality.

MOTHER GRUEL.

If it be so, then he'll be great shortly, for he has no good 285
parts about him.

LETHE.

Well, good woman, or mother, or what you will—

270. my] *Q1;* by *Q2.*
271.] *Dyce; prose* (?) *in Q1–2.*
275. to him] *Q1;* with him *Q2.*
276–277. now . . . you] *Q1* (*cor.*);
I can you now *Q1* (*uncor.*); I can

tell you now *Q2, Dyce seq.*
279. behavior] *Q1* (*cor.*),   *Q2;*
hauiour *Q1* (*uncor.*), *Dyce seq.*
280. His] *Q1* (*cor.*); Hee *Q1*
(*uncor.*), *Q2, Dyce seq.*

276–277. *now . . . you*] Evidently the Q2 compositor and Dyce only
knew the uncorrected state of this forme (cf. ll. 279, 280, and I.ii.17, all
in inner B). The place of *now* in corrected Q1 is preferable, suggesting that
the proofreader consulted MS.—otherwise he would probably have treated
the original error in the same way as Q2.

280. *His*] Price prefers uncorrected *He*; but the emphasis on *virtues* is
borne out by her next sentence (and by analogy to l. 278, where she also
picks up Lethe's last word).

284. *needy quality*] for those who must earn their living.

MOTHER GRUEL.

Alack the day, I know your worship scorns to call me
mother; 'tis not a thing fit for your worship indeed, such a
simple old woman as I am.   290

LETHE.

In pity of thy long journey, there's sixpence British. Tend
upon me, I have business for you.

MOTHER GRUEL.

I'll wait upon your worship.

LETHE.

Two pole off at least.

MOTHER GRUEL.

I am a clean old woman, an't like your worship.   295

LETHE.

It goes not by cleanness here, good woman; if you were
fouler, so you were braver, you might come nearer.   *Exit.*

MOTHER GRUEL.

Nay, and that be the fashion, I hope I shall get it shortly;
there's no woman so old but she may learn, and as an old
lady delights in a young page or monkey, so there are young 300
courtiers will be hungry upon an old woman, I warrant you.

Exit.

[I.ii]

Enter Lethe's pander [Hellgill], *with a* Country Wench.

HELLGILL.

Come, leave your puling and sighing.

COUNTRY WENCH.

Beshrew you now, why did you entice me from my father?

HELLGILL.

Why? To thy better advancement. Wouldst thou, a pretty,

I.ii] *Dyce; no scene division in Q 1–2.*   1. S.P.] *Dyce; Pand[er] Q 1–2 through-*
out scene.

---

291. *sixpence British*] see Introduction, p. x.
291. *Tend*] attend, wait.
294. *pole*] a rod, 5½ yards.
297. *so*] so long as, provided that.
297. *braver*] more richly dressed (Dyce).
[I.ii]
1. *puling*] whining.

beautiful, juicy squall, live in a poor thrum'd house i'th'
country in such servile habiliments, and may well pass for a   5
gentlewoman i'th' city? Does not five hundred do so,
think'st thou, and with worse faces? Oh, now in these latter
days, the devil reigning, 'tis an age for cloven creatures.
But why sad now? Yet indeed 'tis the fashion of any courtesan to be seasick i'th' first voyage, but at next she proclaims   10
open wars, like a beaten soldier. Why, Northamptonshire
lass, dost dream of virginity now? Remember a loose-bodied
gown, wench, and let it go; wires and tires, bents and bums,
felts and falls, thou shalt deceive the world, that gentlewomen indeed shall not be known from others. I have a   15
master to whom I must prefer thee after the aforesaid
decking, Lethe by name, a man of one most admired
property: he can both love thee, and for thy better advancement be thy pander himself, an exc'llent spark of humility.

COUNTRY WENCH.

Well, heaven forgive you, you train me up to't.   20

HELLGILL.

Why, I do acknowledge it, and I think I do you a pleasure
in't.

COUNTRY WENCH.

And if I should prove a harlot now, I should be bound to
curse you.

---

14. thou shalt] *Price conj.;* thou   17. decking] *Q1 (cor.), Q2;* deck-
that shalt *Q1–2, Dyce seq.*   ning *Q1 (uncor.);* deckening *Dyce seq.*

---

4. *squall*] young minx (Cotgrave's *Dictionary of the French and English
Tongues* [1611], s.v., "Obereau," cited in Bullen).
4. *thrum'd*] thatched (Dyce); cf. II.ii.3.
5. *habiliments*] apparel.
8. *cloven*] devilish (since he had cloven hoofs).
11. *beaten*] experienced (Price).
11. *Northamptonshire*] rural county in central England.
12. *loose-bodied*] suggests moral "looseness" (see l. 25); cf. Middleton's
The Family of Love, V.iii.192–193: "a crew of narrow-ruffed, strait-laced,
yet loose-bodied dames."
13–14.] *Wires* were frames for the hair or ruff; *tires*, headdresses; *bents*,
frames to extend dresses at the hips; *bums*, padding about the waist; *felts*,
hats; *falls*, collars.
16. *prefer*] recommend, promote, advance (cf. l. 3).
17. *decking*] dressing up.   18. *property*] attribute, quality.
19. *humility*] since he will share her (Eccles).
23. *bound*] obliged; but he takes it in the sense of "tied."

HELLGILL.

   Bound? Nay, and you prove a harlot, you'll be loose   25
   enough.

COUNTRY WENCH.

   If I had not a desire to go like a gentlewoman, you should be
   hang'd ere you should get me to't, I warrant you.

HELLGILL.

   Nay, that's certain,
   Nor a thousand more of you;   30
   I know you are all chaste enough,
   Till one thing or other tempt you!
   Deny a satin gown and you dare now?

COUNTRY WENCH.

   You know I have no power to do't, and that makes you so
   willful; for what woman is there such a beast that will deny   35
   any thing that is good?

HELLGILL.

   True, they will not, most dissemble.

COUNTRY WENCH.

   No, and she bear a brave mind, she will not, I warrant you.

HELLGILL.

   Why, therefore take heart, faint not at all,
   Women ne'er rise but when they fall;   40
   Let a man break, he's gone, blown up,
   A woman's breaking sets her up;
   Virginity is no city trade,
   You're out o'th' freedom, when you're a maid;
   Down with the lattice, 'tis but thin,   45

29–32.] *this edn.; prose in Q 1–2.*   37. dissemble] *Sampson conj.;* dis-
36. thing] *Q 1 (cor.), Q 2;* things *Q 1*   embler *Q 1–2.*
(uncor.).

---

   33. *Deny*] refuse (Dyce).
   37. *dissemble*] Dyce, Bullen, and Price accept the quarto reading, and
so make him call her a "dissembler" (Dyce glosses *most* as "greatest,
thorough"). But she is being very frank, and they are discussing women in
general (cf. the proverbial notion in Middleton's title, *More Dissemblers
Besides Women*, and in Tilley, T 551, W 710, W 716), hence the emendation
seems necessary.
   41. *break*] default, go bankrupt.
   42. *breaking*] defloration.
   44. *freedom*] city limits or citizenship (see I.i.89, note).

Let coarser beauties work within,
Whom the light mocks; thou art fair and fresh,
The gilded flies will light upon thy flesh.

COUNTRY WENCH.

Beshrew your sweet enchantments, you have won.

HELLGILL [*aside*].

How easily soft women are undone.   50
So farewell wholesome weeds, where treasure pants,
And welcome silks, where lies disease and wants.—
Come, wench, now flow thy fortunes in to bless thee;
I'll bring thee where thou shalt be taught to dress thee.

COUNTRY WENCH.

Oh, as soon as may be! I am in a swoon till I be a gentle-   55
woman; and you know what flesh is man's meat till it be
dress'd—

HELLGILL.

Most certain; no more: a woman.   *Exeunt.*

[II.i]

Enter Rearage, Salewood, Lethe, Easy, *with* Shortyard, *alias* Blastfield,
[*and his* Boy,] *at dice.*

REARAGE.

Gentlemen, I ha' sworn I'll change the room. Dice? Devils!

LETHE.

You see I'm patient, gentlemen.

SALEWOOD.

Ay, the fiend's in't. You're patient, you put up all.

47. and] *Q1; not in Q2.*   56. till] *Q2; tell Q1.*
50. S.D.] *Dyce.*   II.i] *Actus Secundus Q1–2.*
53. in to] *Q1;* into *Q2.*

---

48. *gilded flies*] men with gold.
51. *weeds*] simple country clothing (cf. Induction, l. 2).
51. *treasure*] true happiness (Eccles), or virtue.
51. *pants*] breathes, exists (Dyce), or toils (Price).
57. *dress'd*] Her riddle plays on two senses of the word: to clothe (a
person), and to prepare (food) for the table.
[II.i]
1. *change the room*] for better luck. They are in an "ordinary" or tavern
(Dyce), perhaps The Horn.
3. *put up all*] pocket all the money; also tamely "put up with" any insult
(Price); see l. 55, note, and III.i.113.

REARAGE.

> Come, set me, gentlemen.

SHORTYARD [*to* Easy].

> An Essex gentleman, sir? 5

EASY.

> An unfortunate one, sir.

SHORTYARD.

> I'm bold to salute you, sir. You know not Master Alsup there?

EASY.

> Oh, entirely well.

SHORTYARD.

> Indeed, sir? 10

EASY.

> He's second to my bosom.

SHORTYARD.

> I'll give you that comfort then, sir, you must not want money as long as you are in town, sir.

EASY.

> No, sir?

SHORTYARD.

> I am bound in my love to him to see you furnish'd, and in 15 that comfort I recover my salute again, sir.

EASY.

> Then I desire to be more dear unto you.

SHORTYARD.

> I rather study to be dear unto you. —Boy, fill some wine. —I knew not what fair impressier I receiv'd at first, but I began to affect your society very speedily. 20

EASY.

> I count myself the happier.

5. S.D.] *this edn.*   5. gentleman] *Q2;* genrleman *Q1.*

---

4. *set me*] cover my bet, "fade me."

7. *salute*] probably doffing his hat, which he puts on again at l. 16 (Sampson).

7. *Alsup*] all-sup, suggesting his hospitality (Price).

11. *second*] close, next (Price).

18. *I . . . you*] perhaps an aside (Dyce *seq.*), using *dear* in the sense of "costly" (see Induction, l. 67, note).

19. *impressier*] impressure, impression.

SHORTYARD.

To Master Alsup, sir, to whose remembrance,
I could love to drink till I were past remembrance.   [*Drinks.*]

EASY.

I shall keep Christmas with him, sir, where your health
shall likewise undoubtedly be remember'd, and thereupon   25
I pledge you.   [*Drinks.*]   I would sue for your name, sir.

SHORTYARD.

Your suit shall end in one Term, sir; my name is Blastfield.

EASY.

Kind Master Blastfield, your dearer acquaintance.   [*Drinks.*]

REARAGE.

Nay, come, will ye draw in, gentlemen? Set me.

EASY.

Faith, I'm scatter'd.   30

SHORTYARD.

Sir, you shall not give out so meanly of yourself in my company for a million. Make such privy to your disgrace?
You're a gentleman of fair fortunes; keep me your reputation. Set 'em all; there's crowns for you.

EASY.

Sir, you bind me infinitely in these courtesies.   35

SHORTYARD.

You must always have a care of your reputation here in
town, Master Easy; although you ride down with nothing,
it skills not.

EASY.

I'm glad you tell me that yet, then I'm indifferent. —Well,
come, who throws? I set all these.   40

SHORTYARD.

Why, well said.

SALEWOOD.

This same Master Lethe here begins to undo us again.

22–23.] *this edn.; prose in Q 1–2.*   28. S.D.] *Dyce.*
23. S.D.] *Dyce.*   32. a] *Q 1; not in Q 2.*
26. S.D.] *Dyce.*

---

30. *scatter'd*] broke (Eccles).
32. *such*] such gamesters, men about town (Price).
34. *crowns*] gold coins worth five shillings.
37. *down*] from London to the country (see I.i.253, note).
38. *skills*] signifies (Dyce), matters.

LETHE.

　Ah, sir, I came not hither but to win.

SHORTYARD.

　And then you'll leave us, that's your fashion.

LETHE.

　He's base that visits not his friends.　　　　　　　　　　45

SHORTYARD.

　But he's more base that carries out his winnings;
　None will do so but those have base beginnings.

LETHE.

　It is a thing in use, and ever was.
　I pass this time.

SHORTYARD.　　　　　　I wonder you should pass,
　And that you're suffer'd.

LETHE.　　　　　　　　　Tut, the dice are ours,　　　50
　Then wonder not at those that have most pow'rs.

REARAGE.

　The devil and his angels!

LETHE.　　　　　　　　　Are these they?
　Welcome, dear angels, where y'are curs'd ne'er stay.

　　　　　　　　　　　　　　　　　　　　　[*Retires.*]

SALEWOOD.

　Here's luck!

EASY.

　Let's search him, gentlemen, I think he wears a smock.　　55

53.1.] *Sampson.*

---

　47. *beginnings*] parentage.　　48. *in use*] customary.
　49. *pass*] give up one's turn to shoot the dice.
　50. *suffer'd*] permitted.
　52. *angels*] punning on the coin (see I.i.119, note). Rearage has just lost
again to Lethe, who rakes in the money.
　55. *wears a smock*] see I.i.233, note. Sampson sees a reference to the
saying, "wrapped in's mother's smock" (Tilley, M 1203), meaning "highly
fortunate"; but since this smock is not so specified, probably Easy is just
calling Lethe an effeminate coward for putting up with their insults (cf.
women who are said to "wear the breeches"—Tilley, B 645). Dyce thinks
the phrase means "is a knave"; but his two citations really support this
more obvious reading: the "knaves . . . that wear smocks" in Dekker's
1 Honest Whore (IV.i.183) are simply women disguised as men (cf. 1 *Honest
Whore*, IV.i.126, 184–185); and the statement in John Chamber's *Treatise
Against Judicial Astrology* (1601), p. 113, that "knaves wear smocks" refers to
the traditional reversal of sexual roles during leap year.

SHORTYARD.

I knew the time he wore not half a shirt, just like a pea.

EASY.

No! How did he for the rest?

SHORTYARD.

Faith, he compounded with a couple of napkins at Barnet,
and so truss'd up the lower parts.

EASY.

'Twas a pretty shift, i'faith.   60

SHORTYARD.

But Master Lethe has forgot that too.

EASY.

A mischief on't, to lose all! I could—

SHORTYARD.

Nay, but, good Master Easy, do not do yourself that tyranny,
I beseech you. I must not ha' you alter your body now for
the purge of a little money; you undo me, and you do.   65

EASY.

'Twas all I brought up with me, I protest, Master Blastfield;
all my rent till next quarter.

SHORTYARD.

Pox of money, talk not on't, I beseech you. What said I to
you? Mass, I am out of cash myself too. —Boy!

BOY.

Anon, sir.   70

SHORTYARD.

Run presently to Master Gum the mercer, and will him to

---

56. *pea*] "as nothing between it and the pod, so nothing between Lethe
and his outer garments" (Price).

58. *compounded with*] put together, made do with.

58. *napkins*] probably handkerchiefs (Price).

58. *Barnet*] popular resort town eleven miles northwest of London
(Sugden).

60. *shift*] shirt, and also a clever device (Price).

62. *I could*] Apparently Easy has just lost again, and makes as if to do
himself some bodily harm.

65. *purge*] loss (Price).

66. *up*] to London from Essex (see I.i.253, note).

67. *quarter*] Tenants paid their rent four times a year.

68. *Pox of*] common imprecation; *pox* ("pocks") is syphilis.

70. *Anon*] coming right away.   71. *presently*] immediately.

71. *mercer*] dealer in silks and other fabrics; *gum* was applied to silk to
make it seem glossier (Sampson).

71. *will*] desire (Dyce), ask.

tell out two or three hundred pound for me, or more
according as he is furnish'd. I'll visit him i'th' morning, say.

BOY.

It shall be said, sir.   [*Going.*]

SHORTYARD.

Do you hear, boy?   75

BOY.

Yes, sir.

SHORTYARD.

If Master Gum be not sufficiently ready, call upon Master
Profit the goldsmith.

BOY.

It shall be done, sir.   [*Going.*]

SHORTYARD.

Boy!   80

BOY [*aside*].

I knew I was not sent yet; now is the time.

SHORTYARD.

Let them both rest till another occasion. You shall not need
to run so far at this time; take one nigher hand; go to
Master Quomodo the draper, and will him to furnish me
instantly.   85

BOY.

Now I go, sir.   [*Exit.*]

EASY.

It seems y'are well known, Master Blastfield, and your
credit very spacious here i'th' city.

SHORTYARD.

Master Easy, let a man bear himself portly, the whoresons
will creep to him o'their bellies, and their wives o'their   90
backs; there's a kind of bold grace expected throughout all
the parts of a gentleman. Then, for your observances, a man
must not so much as spit but within line and fashion. I tell

74. S.D.] *Dyce.*   86. S.D.] *Dyce.*
79. S.D.] *Dyce.*   90. o'their . . . o'their] *Dyce* (*subs.*);
81. S.D.] *Dyce.*   a'th their . . . a'th their *Q 1–2.*
81. knew] *Dyce;* know *Q 1–2.*

72. *tell*] count.   83. *nigher hand*] nearer.
88. *spacious*] large, ample.   89. *portly*] imposingly.
89. *whoresons*] sons of whores (i.e., the city merchants).

you what I ha' done: sometimes I carry my water all London
over, only to deliver it proudly at the Standard; and do I   95
pass altogether unnoted, think you? No, a man can no
sooner peep out his head, but there's a bow bent at him
out of some watchtower or other.

EASY.

So readily, sir?

SHORTYARD.

Push, you know a bow's quickly ready, though a gun be long   100
a-charging, and will shoot five times to his once. Come,
you shall bear yourself jovially. Take heed of setting your
looks to your losses, but rather smile upon your ill luck,
and invite 'em tomorrow to another breakfast of bones.

EASY.

Nay, I'll forswear dicing.   105

SHORTYARD.

What? Peace, I am ashamed to hear you; will you cease in
the first loss? Show me one gentleman that e'er did it. Fie
upon't, I must use you to company, I perceive; you'd be
spoil'd else. Forswear dice? I would your friends heard
you, i'faith.   110

EASY.

Nay, I was but in jest, sir.

SHORTYARD.

I hope so, what would gentlemen say of you? "There goes a
gull that keeps his money!" I would not have such a report
go on you for the world, as long as you are in my company.
Why, man, fortune alters in a minute. I ha' known those   115
have recovered so much in an hour, their purses were never
sick after.

REARAGE.

Oh, worse than consumption of the liver!

118–119.] *this edn.; prose in* Q *1–2.*

---

94. *water*] urine.
95. *Standard*] large water fountain in Cheapside (Sugden).
96–101. *No . . . once*] a sustained *double-entendre.*
100. *Push*] pish.
102–103. *setting . . . to*] letting your expression show.
104. *bones*] of which dice were made (cf. l. 127).
108. *use*] accustom.

Consumption of the patrimony!

SHORTYARD.

How now? Mark their humors, Master Easy.   120

REARAGE.

Forgive me, my posterity yet ungotten!

SHORTYARD.

That's a penitent maudlin dicer.

REARAGE.

Few know the sweets that the plain life allows;
Vild son that surfeits of his father's brows!

SHORTYARD.

Laugh at him, Master Easy.   125

EASY.

Hah, hah, hah!

SALEWOOD.

I'll be damn'd, and these be not the bones
Of some quean that cozened me in her life,
And now consumes me after her death.

SHORTYARD.

That's the true wicked, blasphemous, and soul-shuddering 130
dicer, that will curse you all service time, and attribute
his ill luck always to one drab or other.

[*Enter* Hellgill *to* Lethe; *they talk apart.*]

LETHE.

Dick Hellgill, the happy news?

HELLGILL.

I have her for you, sir.

LETHE.

Peace, what is she?   135

HELLGILL.

Young, beautiful, and plump, a delicate piece of sin.

127–129.] *this edn.; prose in Q 1–2.*   132.1.] *Dyce (expanded).*

---

120. *humors*] temperaments, moods.
121. *ungotten*] unborn ("unbegotten").
124. *surfeits . . . brows*] riots on the money earned by the sweat of his
father's brow (Price).
128. *quean*] prostitute.
128. *cozened*] cheated.
131. *service time*] time of church services (Price).

LETHE.

Of what parentage?

HELLGILL.

Oh, a gentlewoman of a great house.

LETHE.

Fie, fie!

HELLGILL [aside].

She newly came out of a barn, yet too good for a tooth- 140
drawer's son.

LETHE.

Is she wife or maid?

HELLGILL.   That which is daintiest, maid.

LETHE.

I'd rather she'd been a wife.

HELLGILL.   A wife, sir? Why?

LETHE.

Oh, adultery is a great deal sweeter
In my mind.

HELLGILL [aside].   Diseases gnaw thy bones!—   145
I think she has deserv'd to be a wife, sir.

LETHE.

That will move well.

HELLGILL.   Her firstlings shall be mine.
Swine look but for the husks; the meat be thine.

[Enter Boy to Shortyard and Easy; they talk apart.]

SHORTYARD.

How now, boy?

138. great] Q1 (cor.); good Q1   144–145. Oh . . . mind] this edn.;
(uncor.), Q2.   prose in Q1–2.
140. S.D.] Dyce.   145. S.D.] Dyce.
                                        148.1.] Dyce (expanded).

---

145. Diseases] syphilis, known as "the bone-ache."

147. move] attract me (Eccles; cf. I.i.223); or, perhaps, move the merchandise (Price; cf. I.ii.18–19).

147–148. Her . . . thine] These lines yield various meanings, none very
convincing, if spoken openly (as in Dyce, Bullen, and Sampson) or in an
aside (as in Schelling and Price), or if only one is an aside (as in Hellgill's
preceding speech). Perhaps mine and thine have been transposed, which
introduces further possibilities; but cf. Shirley's The Lady of Pleasure (II.ii.92–
94), where some panders are said to demand, as their fee, the "first fruits"
of the women they procure for others.

BOY.

> Master Quomodo takes your worship's greeting exceeding 150
> kindly, and in his commendations returns this answer, that
> your worship shall not be so apt to receive it, as he willing
> to lend it.

SHORTYARD.

> Why, we thank him, i'faith.

EASY.

> Troth, and you ha' reason to thank him, sir; 'twas a very 155
> friendly answer.

SHORTYARD.

> Push, a gentleman that keeps his days even here i'th' city,
> as I myself watch to do, shall have many of those answers in
> a twelvemonth, Master Easy.

EASY.

> I promise you, sir, I admire your carriage, and begin to hold 160
> a more rev'rend respect of you.

SHORTYARD.

> Not so, I beseech you, I give my friends leave to be inward
> with me. —Will you walk, gentlemen?

LETHE.

> We're for you.
> [*To* Hellgill.]   Present her with this jewel, my first token.

Enter a Drawer.

DRAWER.

> There are certain countrymen without, inquiring for Master 165
> Rearage and Master Salewood.

REARAGE.

> Tenants!

SALEWOOD.

> Thou reviv'st us, rascal.

REARAGE.

> When's our next meeting, gentlemen?

164. S.D.] *Price.*

---

157. *keeps his days even*] pays his debts on time (Price).
158. *watch*] am careful (Schelling).
160. *carriage*] bearing, style.   162. *inward*] intimate (Dyce).
164.1. *Drawer*] tapster, bartender.
167. *Tenants*] coming to pay their rent.

SHORTYARD.   Tomorrow night;

    This gentleman, by me, invites you all.   170

    Do you not, Master Easy?

EASY.   Freely, sir.

SALEWOOD.

    We do embrace your love. —[*Aside.*] A pure, fresh gull.

SHORTYARD.

    Thus make you men at parting dutiful,

    And rest beholding to you; 'tis the sleight

    To be remember'd when you're out of sight.   175

EASY.

    A pretty virtue.   *Exeunt.*

[II.ii]

    Enter the Country Wench's Father, *that was entic'd for Lethe.*

FATHER.

    Where shall I seek her now? Oh, if she knew

    The dangers that attend on women's lives,

    She would rather lodge under a poor thatch'd roof

    Than under carved ceilings. She was my joy,

    And all content that I receiv'd from life,   5

    My dear and only daughter.

    What says the note she left? Let me again

    With staider grief peruse it.

    [*Reading.*] "Father, wonder not at my so sudden de-

    parture, without your leave or knowledge. Thus, under   10

    pardon, I excuse it: had you had knowledge of it, I know

    you would have sought to restrain it, and hinder me from

    what I have long desir'd. Being now happily prefer'd to a

    gentleman's service in London, about Holborn, if you please

    to send, you may hear well of me."   15

172. S.D.] *Dyce.*   II.ii] *Dyce; no scene division in Q 1–2.*
                                       0.1. *entic'd*] *Q 2; entiic'd Q 1.*

---

174. *rest beholding*] remain obligated, "beholden" (Sampson).

174. *sleight*] trick.

[II.ii]

4. *carved ceilings*] in the homes of the wealthy.

13. *prefer'd*] see I.ii.16, note.

14. *Holborn*] district with a poor reputation (Sugden).

As false as she is disobedient!
I've made larger inquiry, left no place,
Where gentry keeps, unsought, yet cannot hear,
Which drives me most into a shameful fear.
Woe worth th'infected cause that makes me visit   20
This man-devouring city, where I spent
My unshapen youth, to be my age's curse,
And surfeited away my name and state
In swinish riots, that now, being sober,
I do awake a beggar. I may hate her.   25
Whose youth voids wine, his age is curs'd with water.
Oh heavens, I know the price of ill too well,
What the confusions are, in whom they dwell,
And how soon maids are to their ruins won;
One minute, and eternally undone;   30
So in mine may it, may it not be thus!
Though she be poor, her honor's precious.
May be my present form, and her fond fear,
May chase her from me, if her eye should get me;
And therefore, as my love and wants advise,   35
I'll serve, until I find her, in disguise.
Such is my care to fright her from base evils,
I leave calm state to live amongst you, devils.   *Exit.*

[II.iii]

Lethe's Mother *enters with Quomodo's wife* [Thomasine], *with the
letter* [*from Lethe*].

THOMASINE.

Were these fit words, think you, to be sent to any citizen's
wife: to enjoy the daughter, and love the mother too for a

---

33. fond] *Q2;* foud *Q1.*   II.iii] *Dyce; no scene division in Q1–2.*

---

18. *keeps*] dwells (Dyce), frequents.
18. *unsought*] unsearched.
18. *hear*] news of her.
20. *Woe worth*] woe be unto (Sampson).
22. *unshapen*] unformed, undisciplined.
23. *name and state*] good name and estate, inheritance.
26. *voids*] wastes (Price) or vomits.
33. *fond*] foolish.   36. *serve*] become a servant.

need? I would foully scorn that man that should love me
only for a need, I tell you. And here the knave writes again,
that by the marriage of my daughter, 'a has the better means   5
and opportunity to myself. He lies in his throat like a villain,
he has no opportunity of me, for all that; 'tis for his betters
to have opportunity of me, and that he shall well know. A
base, proud knave! 'A has forgot how he came up, and
brought two of his countrymen to give their words to my   10
husband for a suit of green kersey, 'a has forgot all this. And
how does he appear to me when his white satin suit's on,
but like a maggot crept out of a nutshell, a fair body and a
foul neck; those parts that are covered of him looks indifferent well, because we cannot see 'em; else, for all his cleans-   15
ing, pruning, and paring, he's not worthy a broker's
daughter, and so tell him.

MOTHER GRUEL.

I will indeed, forsooth.

THOMASINE.

And as for my child, I hope she'll be rul'd in time, though
she be foolish yet, and not be carried away with a cast of   20
manchets, a bottle of wine, or a custard, and so, I pray,
certify him.

MOTHER GRUEL.

I'll do your errand effectually.

THOMASINE.

Art thou his aunt, or his—

---

5. *'a*] he.

9. *came up*] to London.

10. *countrymen*] perhaps indicating they were foreigners, i.e., Scots
(Maxwell), though the word need not imply this (cf. II.i.165).

10. *give their words*] guarantee his credit.

11. *kersey*] see I.i.238–239, note.

12–14. *how . . . neck*] cf. Webster's *The White Devil*, I.ii.136–137 (ed.
Lucas, who notes the borrowing).

16. *broker*] a contemptuous term applied to various kinds of petty dealers
or agents (cf. l. 382).

20–21. *cast of manchets*] a few small loaves or rolls of fine white bread
(Dyce).

22. *certify*] assure (Schelling).

24. *aunt*] cant term for "bawd," which Mother Gruel apparently
does not understand (cf. III.i.240).

MOTHER GRUEL.

    Alas, I am a poor drudge of his. 25

THOMASINE.

    Faith, and thou wert his mother, he would make thee his
drudge, I warrant him.

MOTHER GRUEL.

    Marry, out upon him, sir-reverence of your mistress-ship.

THOMASINE.

    Here's somewhat for thy pains, fare thee well.   [*Giving money.*]

MOTHER GRUEL.

    'Tis more than he gave me since I came to him.   [*Exit.*] 30

      Enter Quomodo *and his daughter* Su[san].

QUOMODO.

    How now, what prating have we here? Whispers? Dumb
shows? Why, Thomasine, go to; my shop is not altogether
so dark as some of my neighbors', where a man may be
made cuckold at one end, while he's measuring with his
yard at tother. 35

THOMASINE.

    Only commendations sent from Master Lethe, your worship-
ful son-in-law that should be.

QUOMODO.

    Oh, and that you like not. He that can make us rich in
custom, strong in friends, happy in suits, bring us into all the
rooms o'Sundays, from the leads to the cellar, pop us in with 40
venison till we crack again, and send home the rest in an
honorable napkin; this man you like not, forsooth!

SUSAN.

    But I like him, father.

29. S.D.] *Dyce*.   30. S.D.] *Dyce*.

---

   28. *sir-reverence*] begging your pardon (originally, "saving your reverence")
for the vulgarity.

   31–32. *Dumb shows*] pantomimes.

   32–35. *my . . . yard*] see Dramatis Personae, ll. 7–8, note, and I.i.85–89,
note. The scene is located in Quomodo's shop (Dyce).

   35. *tother*] the other.

   39. *custom*] trade (Price).

   39. *happy in suits*] fortunate in our petitions at Court (Eccles; cf. I.i.168).

   39–40. *bring . . . rooms*] show us through the Court.

   40. *leads*] roof (Schelling).

QUOMODO.

My blessing go with thy liking.

SUSAN.

A number of our citizens hold our credit by't, to come   45
home drunk, and say we ha' been at Court; then how much
more credit is't to be drunk there indeed!

QUOMODO.

Tut, thy mother's a fool. —Pray, what's Master Rearage
whom you plead for so?

THOMASINE.

Why, first, he is a gentleman.   50

QUOMODO.

Ay, he's often first a gentleman that's last a beggar.

SUSAN.

My father tells you true. What should I do with a
gentleman? I know not which way to lie with him.

QUOMODO.

'Tis true, too. Thou know'st, beside, we undo gentlemen
daily.   55

THOMASINE.

That makes so few of 'em marry with our daughters, unless
it be one green fool or other. Next, Master Rearage has land
and living, tother but his walk i'th' street, and his snatching
diet; he's able to entertain you in a fair house of his own,
tother in some nook or corner, or place us behind the   60
cloth like a company of puppets; at his house you shall
be serv'd curiously, sit down and eat your meat with leisure;
there we must be glad to take it standing, and without either
salt, cloth, or trencher, and say we are befriended too.

57. fool] *Q2;* foote *Q1.*

---

45. *credit*] reputation, prestige.
57. *green*] raw, inexperienced.   58. *living*] rent from his lands.
58–59. *snatching diet*] whatever he can lay hands on (Eccles); or eaten
"on the run" (see the following quotation).
61. *cloth*] the arras (tapestry) at Court. Cf. Beaumont and Fletcher's
The Woman-Hater, III.iv: "my fellow Courtiers all, with whom,/ I have
of yore made many a scrambling meal/ In corners, behind Arasses, on
stairs."
61. *puppets*] i.e., before the curtain rose (Eccles).
62. *curiously*] elaborately, solicitously.
63. *there*] at Court.   64. *trencher*] wooden platter.

QUOMODO.

Oh, that gives a citizen a better appetite than his garden.   65

SUSAN.

So say I, father; methinks it does me most good when I take it standing, I know not how all women's minds are.

Enter Falselight.

QUOMODO.

Faith, I think they are all of thy mind for that thing. —How now, Falselight?

FALSELIGHT.

I have descried my fellow, Shortyard, alias Blastfield, at   70 hand with the gentleman.

QUOMODO.

Oh, my sweet Shortyard! —Daughter, get you up to your virginals.   [*Exit* Susan.]

By your leave, Mistress Quomodo—

THOMASINE.

Why, I hope I may sit i'th' shop, may I not?   75

QUOMODO.

That you may, and welcome, sweet honey-thigh, but not at this season; there's a buck to be struck.

THOMASINE [*aside*].

Well, since I'm so expressly forbidden, I'll watch above i'th' gallery, but I'll see your knavery.   *Exit.*

QUOMODO.

Be you prepar'd as I tell you.   80

FALSELIGHT.

You ne'er fear'd me.   *Exit.*

QUOMODO.

Oh, that sweet, neat, comely, proper, delicate parcel of land,

73. S.D.] *Dyce.*   78. S.D.] *Dyce.*

---

65. *garden*] Many Londoners had small vegetable gardens.
66–67.] a *double-entendre.*
73. *virginals*] a kind of spinet (Dyce).
74. *By your leave*] Please leave us (Price).
77. *season*] time.
77. *buck to be struck*] deer (victim) to be brought down.
81. *fear'd me*] feared for me, lest I slip (Price).
82. *proper*] excellent, handsome.

like a fine gentlewoman i'th' waist, not so great as pretty,
pretty; the trees in summer whistling, the silver waters by
the banks harmoniously gliding. I should have been a   85
scholar; an excellent place for a student, fit for my son that
lately commenc'd at Cambridge, whom now I have plac'd at
Inns of Court. Thus we that seldom get lands honestly, must
leave our heirs to inherit our knavery.   But whist, one turn
about my shop and meet with 'em.   90

Enter Master Easy *with* Shortyard, *alias* Blastfield, [*and his* Boy].

EASY.

Is this it, sir?

SHORTYARD.

Ay, let me see, this is it; sign of Three Knaves, 'tis it.

QUOMODO [*into the shop*].

Do you hear, sir? —What lack you, gentlemen? See good
kerseys or broadcloths here; I pray come near. —Master
Blastfield!   95

SHORTYARD.

I thought you would know me anon.

[*Enter* Thomasine *above*.]

QUOMODO.

You're exceeding welcome to town, sir. Your worship must
pardon me, 'tis always misty weather in our shops here; we
are a nation the sun ne'er shines upon. Came this gentleman
with you?   100

93. S.D.] *this edn.*   96.1.] *Dyce;* "*Tomazin aboue*" *Q 1–2*
                                 (*after l. 201*).

---

86. *scholar*] because he can speak so "poetically."
87. *commenc'd*] graduated.
88. *Inns of Court*] residence halls for law students.
89. *whist*] hush (Bullen).
92. *Three Knaves*] Quomodo, Shortyard, Falselight (parodying the sign-
boards hung outside shops to identify them).
93. S.D.] He pretends to give orders to someone within, so that he
will not seem to be expecting them.
93. *What lack you*] a shopkeeper's usual greeting (Sampson).
96.1. *above*] the upper stage (*gallery*, l. 79), where she observes the action
below without being seen.
98. *misty weather*] cf. ll. 32–33.

SHORTYARD.

Oh, salute him fairly, he's a kind gentleman, a very inward of mine.

QUOMODO.

Then I cry you mercy, sir, y'are especially welcome.

EASY.

I return you thanks, sir.

QUOMODO.

But how shall I do for you now, Master Blastfield?   105

SHORTYARD.

Why, what's the matter?

QUOMODO.

It is my greatest affliction at this instant, I am not able to furnish you.

SHORTYARD.

How, Master Quomodo? Pray, say not so; 'slud, you undo me then.   110

QUOMODO.

Upon my religion, Master Blastfield, bonds lie forfeit in my hands; I expect the receipt of a thousand every hour, and cannot yet set eye of a penny.

SHORTYARD.

That's strange, methinks.

QUOMODO.

'Tis mine own pity that plots against me, Master Blastfield; 115 they know I have no conscience to take the forfeiture, and that makes 'em so bold with my mercy.

EASY.

I am sorry for this.

QUOMODO.

Nevertheless, if I might entreat your delay but the age of three days, to express my sorrow now, I would double the 120 sum, and supply you with four or five hundred.

116. the] *Q1; not in Q2.*

---

101. *inward*] intimate friend (Dyce; cf. II.i.162).
103. *cry you mercy*] beg your pardon.
109. *'slud*] common oath, "God's blood."
111. *bonds lie forfeit*] debts are overdue.
116. *take the forfeiture*] foreclose.

SHORTYARD.

Let me see, three days?

QUOMODO.

Ay, good sir, and it may be possible.

EASY.

Do you hear, Master Blastfield?   [*Taking him aside.*]

SHORTYARD.

Hah?   125

EASY.

You know I've already invited all the gallants to sup with
me tonight.

SHORTYARD.

That's true, i'faith.

EASY.

'Twill be my everlasting shame, if I have no money to
maintain my bounty.   130

SHORTYARD.

I ne'er thought upon that. —[*Aside.*] I look'd still when that
should come from him. —We have strictly examined our
expenses; it must not be three days, Master Quomodo.

QUOMODO.

No? Then I'm afraid 'twill be my grief, sir.

EASY.

Master Blastfield, I'll tell you what you may do now.   135

SHORTYARD.

What, good sweet bedfellow?

EASY.

Send to Master Gum or Master Profit, the mercer and goldsmith.

SHORTYARD.

Mass, that was well remember'd of thee. —[*Aside.*] I
perceive the trout will be a little troublesome ere he be   140
catch'd. —Boy!

124. S.D.] *this edn.*   *Q2;* Mister . . . Mister *Q1* (*uncor.*).
131. S.D.] *Dyce.*   137. Gum] *Dyce;* Goome *Q1–2.*
137. Master . . . Master] *Q1* (*cor.*),   139. S.D.] *Dyce.*

130. *bounty*] hospitality.
131–132. *I look'd . . . come*] I was waiting to hear that (Sampson).
136. *bedfellow*] see I.i.127, note.

BOY.

    Here, sir.

SHORTYARD.

    Run to Master Gum, or Master Profit, and carry my
present occasion of money to 'em.

BOY.

    I run, sir.   [*Exit.*] 145

QUOMODO.

    Methinks, Master Blastfield, you might easily attain to the
satisfaction of three days; here's a gentleman, your friend,
I dare say will see you sufficiently possess'd till then.

EASY.

    Not I, sir, by no means; Master Blastfield knows I'm further
in want than himself. My hope rests all upon him; it stands 150
upon the loss of my credit tonight, if I walk without money.

SHORTYARD.

    Why, Master Quomodo, what a fruitless motion have you
put forth! You might well assure yourself this gentleman
had it not, if I wanted it. Why, our purses are brothers; we
desire but equal fortunes; in a word, w'are man and wife; 155
they can but lie together, and so do we.

EASY.

    As near as can be, i'faith.

SHORTYARD.

    And to say truth, 'tis more for the continuing of this
gentleman's credit in town, than any incitement from mine
own want only, that I covet to be so immediately furnish'd. 160
You shall hear him confess as much himself.

EASY.

    'Tis most certain, Master Quomodo.

                   Enter Boy.

SHORTYARD.

    Oh, here comes the boy now. —How now, boy, what says
Master Gum, or Master Profit?

143. Gum] *Dyce;* Goome *Q 1–2.*   164. Gum] *Dyce;* Goome *Q 1–2.*
145. S.D.] *Dyce.*

  143–144. *carry . . . occasion*] convey my immediate need.
  150–151. *stands upon*] involves.   151. *walk*] depart (Dyce).
  152. *motion*] proposal (Price).
  160. *covet*] strongly desire.

BOY.

Sir, they're both walk'd forth this frosty morning to Brain- 165
ford, to see a nurse-child.

SHORTYARD.

A bastard be it! Spite and shame!

EASY.

Nay, never vex yourself, sweet Master Blastfield.

SHORTYARD.

Bewitch'd, I think!

QUOMODO.

Do you hear, sir? [*Taking* Easy *aside.*] You can persuade 170
with him?

EASY.

A little, sir.

QUOMODO.

Rather than he should be altogether destitute, or be too
much a vexation to himself, he shall take up a commodity
of cloth of me, tell him.   175

EASY.

Why, la! By my troth, 'twas kindly spoken.

QUOMODO.

Two hundred pound's worth, upon my religion, say.

SHORTYARD.

So disastrously!

EASY.

Nay, Master Blastfield, you do not hear what Master Quomodo said since, like an honest, true citizen, i'faith. Rather 180
than you should grow diseas'd upon't, you shall take up a
commodity of two hundred pound's worth of cloth.

SHORTYARD.

The mealy moth consume it! Would he ha' me turn peddler
now? What should I do with cloth?

170. S.D.] *this edn.*

165–166. *Brainford*] Brentford, a town eight miles west of London, a
favorite resort for a day's excursion (Sugden).

166. *nurse-child*] infant lodged away from home with a wet-nurse. This
was done with children of respectable families but was also a means of
concealing illegitimate births.

174. *take . . . commodity*] take the loan in goods in lieu of cash (see
Introduction, p. xiv).

181. *diseas'd*] dis-eased, worried (Price).   183. *mealy*] spotted, flecked.

QUOMODO.

He's a very willful gentleman at this time, i'faith. He knows 185
as well what to do with it as I myself, iwis. There's no
merchant in town but will be greedy upon't, and pay down
money upo'th' nail; they'll dispatch it over to Middleborrow presently, and raise double commodity by exchange.

If not, you know 'tis Term-time, and Michaelmas Term too, 190
the drapers' harvest for footcloths, riding-suits, walking-
suits, chamber gowns, and hall gowns.

EASY.

Nay, I'll say that, it comes in as fit a time as can be.

QUOMODO.

Nay, take me with you again ere you go, sir; I offer him no
trash, tell him, but present money, say, where I know some 195
gentlemen in town ha' been glad, and are glad at this time,
to take up commodities in hawks' hoods and brown paper.

EASY.

Oh, horrible! Are there such fools in town?

QUOMODO.

I offer him no trash, tell him, upon my religion, you may say.
—[*Aside*.] Now, my sweet Shortyard; now the hungry fish 200
begins to nibble; one end of the worm is in his mouth, i'faith.

THOMASINE [*aside*].

Why stand I here (as late our graceless dames

200. S.D.] *Dyce*.   202. S.D.] *Dyce*.

---

185. *willful*] obstinate, contrary.   186. *iwis*] certainly.

188. *upo'th' nail*] at once, on the spot (Tilley, N 18); cf. "cash on the
barrelhead."

188–189. *Middleborrow*] Middleburgh, a Dutch port and center of
international trade (Sugden).

189. *raise . . . exchange*] get twice its value in trade.

191. *harvest*] for "reaping" profits.

191. *footcloths*] long ornate cloths draped over a horse's back, used by
men of distinction.

192. *chamber gowns, and hall gowns*] gowns for home or office wear, and
gowns for ceremonial use (Sampson).

194. *take . . . you*] understand me fully (Dyce).

195. *where*] whereas (Dyce).

197. *hoods*] Hunting hawks were kept hooded until let loose on their
prey.

202–205.] She compares herself to women watching a public execution
(see ll. 341–343, and Introduction, p. x).

That found no eyes) to see that gentleman
Alive, in state and credit, executed,
Help to rip up himself, does all he can?   205
Why am I wife to him that is no man?
I suffer in that gentleman's confusion.

EASY.

Nay, be persuaded in that, Master Blastfield; 'tis ready
money at the merchants'; beside, the winter season and all
falls in as pat as can be to help it.   210

SHORTYARD.

Well, Master Easy, none but you could have persuaded me
to that. —Come, would you would dispatch then, Master
Quomodo; where's this cloth?

QUOMODO.

Full and whole within, all of this piece, of my religion,
Master Blastfield. Feel't, nay, feel't and spare not, gentle- 215
men; your fingers and your judgment.

SHORTYARD.

Cloth's good.

EASY.

By my troth, exceeding good cloth; a good wale 't'as.

QUOMODO.

Falselight!

[*Enter* Falselight.]

FALSELIGHT.

I'm ne'er out o'the shop, sir.   220

QUOMODO.

Go, call in a porter presently to carry away the cloth with
the star mark. —Whither will you please to have it carried,
Master Blastfield?

SHORTYARD.

Faith, to Master Beggarland, he's the only merchant

219.1.] *this edn.*

---

203. *no eyes*] to weep (Eccles).
205.] i.e., does all he can to help the executioner disembowel him (a
stage in the execution for treason).
207. *confusion*] ruin.   212. *dispatch*] settle it quickly.
218. *wale*] texture (Dyce).
220.] playing on the meaning of his name.
222. *star mark*] a pattern (Price), or coded label.

now; or his brother, Master Stilliard-down, there's little 225
difference.

QUOMODO.

Y'ave happen'd upon the money men, sir; they and some of
their brethren, I can tell you, will not stick to offer thirty
thousand pound to be curs'd still; great monied men,
their stocks lie in the poor's throats. But you'll see me suffi- 230
ciently discharg'd, Master Blastfield, ere you depart?

SHORTYARD.

You have always found me righteous in that.

QUOMODO.

Falselight!

FALSELIGHT.

Sir?

QUOMODO.

You may bring a scrivener along with you.   235

FALSELIGHT.

I'll remember that, sir.   [*Exit.*]

QUOMODO.

Have you sent for a citizen, Master Blastfield?

SHORTYARD.

No, faith, not yet. —Boy!

EASY.

What must you do with a citizen, sir?

SHORTYARD.

A custom they're bound to a-late by the default of evil 240
debtors; no citizen must lend money without two be bound
in the bond; the second man enters but for custom sake.

EASY.

No? And must he needs be a citizen?

229. men] *Q1;* mee *Q2.*   discharged *Q1* (*uncor.*).
231. discharg'd] *Q1* (*cor.*), *Q2;*   236. S.D.] *Dyce.*

---

225. *brother*] another of that type (cf. *brethren,* l. 228).
225. *Stilliard-down*] "false balance" (Sampson); a "steelyard" was a
scale for weighing.
228. *stick*] scruple, hesitate.   229. *still*] continually (Schelling).
231. *discharg'd*] released, by signing a promissory note (*bond,* l. 242)
for the loan.
235. *scrivener*] see Dramatis Personae, l. 12, note.
241. *without*] unless.

SHORTYARD.

By th' mass, stay, I'll learn that. —Master Quomodo!

QUOMODO.

Sir?   245

SHORTYARD.

Must the second party, that enters into bond only for
fashion's sake, needs be a citizen? What say you to this
gentleman for one?

QUOMODO.

Alas, sir, you know he's a mere stranger to me; I neither am
sure of his going or abiding; he may inn here tonight, and 250
ride away tomorrow. Although I grant the chief burden lies
upon you, yet we are bound to make choice of those we
know, sir.

SHORTYARD.

Why, he's a gentleman of a pretty living, sir.

QUOMODO.

It may be so, yet, under both your pardons, I'd rather 255
have a citizen.

EASY.

I hope you will not disparage me so. 'Tis well known I have
three hundred pound a year in Essex.

SHORTYARD.

Well said! To him thyself, take him up roundly.

EASY.

And how doubtfully so e'er you account of me, I do not think 260
but I might make my bond pass for a hundred pound i'th'
city.

QUOMODO.

What, alone, sir?

248. gentleman] *Dyce;* genleman   249. a . . . neither] *Q1 (cor.), Q2;*
Q1–2 (gentleman *in catchword*).   a stranger to me, I meere neither
                                        Q1 (uncor.).

---

250. *inn*] see I.i.41, note.
251. *chief burden*] since Easy is only the guarantor or undersigner (but
see ll. 325–336).
258. *three . . . Essex*] in rent (his *living*, l. 254).
259. *roundly*] bluntly, unsparingly, thoroughly.
260. *how . . . e'er*] however doubtfully.

EASY.

> Alone, sir? Who says so? Perhaps I'd send down for a
> tenant or two.   265

QUOMODO.

> Ay, that's another case, sir.

EASY.

> Another case let it be then!

QUOMODO.

> Nay, grow not into anger, sir.

EASY.

> Not take me into a bond? As good as you shall, goodman
> goosecap.   270

QUOMODO.

> Well, Master Blastfield, because I will not disgrace the
> gentleman, I'm content for once, but we must not make a
> practice on't.

EASY.

> No, sir, now you would, you shall not.

QUOMODO [*aside*].

> Cuds me, I'm undone; he's gone again.   275

SHORTYARD [*aside*].

> The net's broke.

THOMASINE [*aside*].

> Hold there, dear gentleman.

EASY.

> Deny me that small courtesy? 'Sfoot, a very Jew will not
> deny it me.

SHORTYARD [*aside*].

> Now must I catch him warily.   280

EASY.

> A jest indeed! Not take me into a bond, quo' they.

SHORTYARD.

> Master Easy.   [*Taking him aside.*]   Mark my words, if it

275. S.D.] *Dyce.*	280. S.D.] *Dyce.*
276. S.D.] *Dyce.*	282. S.D.] *this edn.*
277. S.D.] *Dyce.*	

---

264. *down*] to his estate in Essex.   270. *goosecap*] booby (Sampson).
275. *Cuds me*] mild oath, originally "God save me."
277. *Hold there*] stick to that.   278. *'Sfoot*] oath, "God's foot."
281. *quo' they*] quoth (said) they, forsooth, indeed.

stood not upon the eternal loss of thy credit against supper—

EASY.

Mass, that's true.

SHORTYARD.

The pawning of thy horse for his own vittles—   285

EASY.

Right, i'faith.

SHORTYARD.

And thy utter dissolution amongst gentlemen forever—

EASY.

Pox on't!

SHORTYARD.

Quomodo should hang, rot, stink—

QUOMODO [*aside*].

Sweet boy, i'faith.   290

SHORTYARD.

Drop, damn.

QUOMODO [*aside*].

Excellent Shortyard!

EASY.

I forgot all this; what meant I to swagger before I had money in my purse? —How does Master Quomodo? Is the bond ready?   295

QUOMODO.

Oh, sir!

Enter Dustbox, *the scrivener.*

EASY.

Come, we must be friends; here's my hand.

QUOMODO.

Give it the scrivener; here he comes.

DUSTBOX.

Good day, Master Quomodo. Good morrow, gentlemen.

283. stood] *Q1;* shood *Q2.*   291. Drop, damn] *Dyce;* Drop Dam
289. should] *Q1;* shall *Q2.*   *Q1–2.*
290. S.D.] *Dyce.*   292. S.D.] *Dyce.*

---

285. *vittles*] cost of his board (victuals); see III.v.29–30, note.
291. *damn*] be damned (Price); the text may be corrupt.
297. *hand*] to shake; but Quomodo takes the word in the sense of "handwriting" or "signature" (cf. l. 346).

QUOMODO.

We must require a little aid from your pen, good Master   300
Dustbox.

DUSTBOX.

What be the gentlemen's names that are bound, sir?

QUOMODO.

Master John Blastfield, esquire, i'th' wild of Kent, and—
what do they call your bedfellow's name?

SHORTYARD.

Master Richard Easy; you may easily hit on't.   305

QUOMODO.

Master Richard Easy, of Essex, gentleman; both bound to
Ephestian Quomodo, citizen and draper, of London; the
sum, two hundred pound. —What time do you take,
Master Blastfield, for the payment?

SHORTYARD.

I never pass my month, you know.   310

QUOMODO.

I know it, sir. October sixteenth today; sixteenth of
November, say.

EASY.

Is it your custom to return so soon, sir?

SHORTYARD.

I never miss you.

Enter Falselight, *like a porter, sweating.*

FALSELIGHT.

I am come for the rest of the same piece, Master Quomodo. 315

QUOMODO.

Star mark, this is it. Are all the rest gone?

---

311. I . . . sir] *Dyce; separate line in*   315. piece] *Bullen* (*Dyce conj.*);
Q 1–2.   price *Q 1–2.*

---

303. *Kent*] county southeast of London; the *wild* (Weald) was a district
in it (Sugden).

313. *return*] render back, repay (Price).

314.1. *like*] disguised as.

315. *piece*] cf. l. 214. Price rejects this emendation on the ground that a
compositor's misreading of "piece" (in Middleton's handwriting) as
"price" would be unlikely; but the identical error occurs in *No Wit, No
Help Like a Woman's*, I.ii.49, where "piece" must be the true reading.

FALSELIGHT.

They're all at Master Stilliard-down's by this time.

EASY.

How the poor rascal's all in a froth!

SHORTYARD.

Push, they're ordain'd to sweat for gentlemen;

Porters' backs and women's bellies bear up the world.   320

[*Exit* Falselight *with cloth.*]

EASY.

'Tis true, i'faith; they bear men and money, and that's the world.

SHORTYARD.

Y'ave found it, sir.

DUSTBOX.

I'm ready to your hands, gentlemen.   [*Presenting bond.*]

SHORTYARD.

Come, Master Easy.   [*Offering to let him sign first.*] 325

EASY.

I beseech you, sir.

SHORTYARD.

It shall be yours, I say.

EASY.

Nay, pray, Master Blastfield.

SHORTYARD.

I will not, i'faith.

EASY.

What do you mean, sir?   330

SHORTYARD.

I should show little bringing up, to take the way of a stranger.

EASY.

By my troth, you do yourself wrong though, Master Blastfield.

320.1.] *Dyce (subs.)*.   325. S.D.] *this edn.*
324. S.D.] *this edn.*   333. S.P.] *Q1 (Eas); Fals Q2.*

---

323. *it*] my meaning, the answer to my riddle.
327. *It*] the "honor" of signing first.
331. *take the way of*] precede.

SHORTYARD.

  Not a whit, sir.   335

EASY.

  But to avoid strife, you shall have your will of me for once.

SHORTYARD.

  Let it be so, I pray.

QUOMODO [aside, while Easy signs].

  Now I begin to set one foot upon the land. Methinks I am
  felling of trees already; we shall have some Essex logs yet to
  keep Christmas with, and that's a comfort.   340

THOMASINE [aside].

  Now is he quart'ring out; the executioner
  Strides over him; with his own blood he writes.

  I am no dame that can endure such sights.   Exit [above].

SHORTYARD [aside].

  So his right wing is cut; he will not fly far
  Past the two city hazards, Poultry and Wood Street.   345

EASY.

  How like you my Roman hand, i'faith?

DUSTBOX.

  Exceeding well, sir, but that you rest too much upon your
  R's, and make your E's too little.

EASY.

  I'll mend that presently.

335.] *Q1; Q2 repeats l. 337.*	344. he] *Q1 (cor.); not in Q1*
338. S.D.] *Dyce (subs.).*	*(uncor.), Q2.*
341. S.D.] *Dyce.*	348. R's] *Sampson;* R. *Q1–2.*
344. S.D.] *Dyce.*	348. E's] *Schelling;* ease *Q1–2.*

  340. *keep Christmas*] with the traditional Yule log (Dyce).

  341. *quart'ring out*] being quartered (Sampson), the last stage in an
execution for treason.

  342. *own blood*] since he is signing away his inheritance, his lifeblood
(Price).

  344. *he*] Price thinks the uncorrected state is more typical of Middleton.
The proofreader may not have consulted MS. here.

  345. *Poultry and Wood Street*] London "Counters," prisons for debtors.

  346. *Roman hand*] The "Roman" or "Italian" style of handwriting was
replacing the native "English" script (Price).

  348. *R's . . . E's*] This emendation (to recover the puns on "arse" and
"ease") was first suggested by K. Deighton, *The Old Dramatists: Conjectural
Readings* (London, 1896), p. 168, and was adopted in W. H. Williams'
Specimens of the Elizabethan Drama (Oxford, 1905), which reprints part of
this scene.

DUSTBOX.

Nay, 'tis done now, past mending.   [Shortyard *signs*.]   You   350
both deliver this to Master Quomodo as your deed?

SHORTYARD.

We do, sir.

QUOMODO.

I thank you, gentlemen.   [*Exit* Dustbox.]

SHORTYARD.

Would the coin would come away now! We have deserv'd
for't.   355

Enter Falselight, [*like a porter*,] *with the cloth*.

FALSELIGHT.

By your leave a little, gentlemen.

SHORTYARD.

How now? What's the matter? Speak!

FALSELIGHT.

As fast as I can, sir. All the cloth's come back again.

QUOMODO.

How?

SHORTYARD.

What's the news?   360

FALSELIGHT.

The passage to Middleborrow is stop'd, and therefore
neither Master Stilliard-down nor Master Beggarland, nor
any other merchant, will deliver present money upon't.

QUOMODO.

Why, what hard luck have you, gentlemen!   [*Exit* Falselight.]

EASY.

Why, Master Blastfield!   365

350. S.D.] *Dyce (subs.).*
353. S.D.] *Price.*

355.1. Falselight] *Q1 (cor.)*, *Q2;*
Flaslight Q1 (uncor.).
364. S.D.] *Dyce.*

---

353. S.D.] Perhaps by oversight, Dyce *seq.* provide no exit for Dustbox
before the general one at l. 437.1.

354. *coin*] money for the cloth.

356. *By . . . little*] Please make way a little.

361. *passage*] route, crossing (of the English Channel).

361. *stop'd*] perhaps by a Spanish blockade (Sampson), or by an edict
of the English government prohibiting export (Eccles).

SHORTYARD.

Pish!

EASY.

You're so discontented too presently, a man cannot tell how to speak to you.

SHORTYARD.

Why, what would you say?

EASY.

We must make somewhat on't now, sir.   370

SHORTYARD.

Ay, where? How? The best is, it lies all upon my neck. —Master Quomodo, can you help me to any money for't? Speak.

QUOMODO.

Troth, Master Blastfield, since myself is so unfurnish'd, I know not the means how. There's one i'th' street, a new 375 setter-up; if any lay out money upon't, 'twill be he.

SHORTYARD.

His name?

QUOMODO.

Master Idem. But you know we cannot give but greatly to your loss, because we gain and live by't.

SHORTYARD.

'Sfoot, will he give anything?   380

EASY.

Ay, stand upon that.

SHORTYARD.

Will he give anything? The brokers will give nothing, to no purpose.

QUOMODO.

Falselight!

[*Enter* Falselight *above.*]

384.1.] *Dyce.*

375–376. *new setter-up*] newly set up in the trade.

378. *Idem*] "the same"; so named, as Price notes, because he is a fiction for Quomodo himself (cf. l. 438).

378–379. *we . . . loss*] Our "buying" price for goods must be much lower than our "selling" price (which you just paid).

381. *stand*] insist.

382. *brokers*] probably pawnbrokers (Price).

FALSELIGHT.

Over your head, sir.   385

QUOMODO.

Desire Master Idem to come presently and look upo'th'
cloth.

FALSELIGHT.

I will, sir.   [*Exit above.*]

SHORTYARD.

What if he should offer but a hundred pound?

EASY.

If he want twenty on't, let's take it.   390

SHORTYARD.

Say you so?

EASY.

Master Quomodo will have four or five hundred pound for
you of his own within three or four days.

[*Enter* Thomasine.]

SHORTYARD.

'Tis true, he said so indeed.

EASY.

Is that your wife, Master Quomodo?   395

QUOMODO.

That's she, little Thomasine!

EASY.

Under your leave, sir, I'll show myself a gentleman.

QUOMODO.

Do, and welcome, Master Easy.

EASY.

I have commission for what I do, lady, from your husband.

[*Kisses her.*]

THOMASINE.

You may have a stronger commission for the next, an't   400
please you, that's from myself.

388. S.D.] *Dyce.*   393.1.] *Dyce.*
392. will] *Q1* (*cor.*); we wil *Q1*   399.1.] *Dyce.*
(*uncor.*); he wil *Q2, Dyce seq.*

---

385. *Over your head*] another play on his name.
390. *want twenty on't*] offer only eighty pounds.
397. *show myself*] by kissing her, the usual salutation.

Enter Sim.

EASY.

You teach me the best law, lady.

THOMASINE [*aside*].

Beshrew my blood, a proper springall and a sweet gentleman.

QUOMODO.

My son, Sim Quomodo! Here's more work for you, Master 405
Easy; you must salute him too— [*aside*] for he's like to be
heir of thy land, I can tell thee.

SIM.

Vim, vitam, spemque salutem.

QUOMODO.

He shows you there he was a Cambridge man, sir, but now
he's a Templar. Has he not good grace to make a lawyer? 410

EASY.

A very good grace to make a lawyer.

SHORTYARD [*aside*].

For, indeed, he has no grace at all.

QUOMODO.

Some gave me counsel to make him a divine—

EASY.

Fie, fie!

QUOMODO.

But some of our Livery think it an unfit thing, that our 415
own sons should tell us of our vices; others, to make him a
physician, but then, being my heir, I'm afraid he would
make me away; now, a lawyer, they're all willing to, because

---

403. S.D.] *Dyce.*
403. proper springall] *Dyce;* proper,
springfull, *Q1–2.*
406. S.D.] *Dyce.*

408. *spemque*] *Q2* (*spemᵭ*); *sprinᵭ*
Q1.
409. but] *Q1; not in Q2.*
412. S.D.] *Dyce.*

---

403. *springall*] youth (Dyce); a variant of "springald."
404.] Dyce *seq.* have her exit here, which seems unnecessary.
408.] "Let me salute vigor, life, and hope." The awkward Latin may
be intended to show Sim's ignorance (Price).
410. *Templar*] at one of the Inns of Court (l. 88).
415. *Livery*] the Woolen Drapers' Company. Each of the great London
guilds had its distinctive ceremonial robes or "livery."
418. *make me away*] make away with me, kill me.

'tis good for our trade, and increaseth the number of cloth
gowns, and indeed 'tis the fittest for a citizen's son, for our 420
word is, "What do ye lack?" and their word is, "What do
you give?"

EASY.

Exceeding proper.

Enter Falselight *for Master Idem.*

QUOMODO.

Master Idem, welcome.

FALSELIGHT.

I have seen the cloth, sir.   425

QUOMODO.

Very well.

FALSELIGHT.

I am but a young setter-up; the uttermost I dare venture
upon't is three-score pound.

SHORTYARD.

What?

FALSELIGHT.

If it be for me, so, I am for it; if not, you have your cloth 430
and I have my money.

EASY.

Nay, pray, Master Blastfield, refuse not his kind offer.

SHORTYARD.

A bargain then, Master Idem, clap hands. —[*Aside.*] He's
finely cheated. —Come, let's all to the next tavern and see
the money paid.   435

EASY.

A match!

QUOMODO.

I follow you, gentlemen; take my son along with you.

                            Exeunt [*all but* Quomodo].

Now to my keys; I'm Master Idem, he must fetch the money.

433. S.D.] *Dyce.*

---

420. *gowns*] worn by lawyers (cf. Induction, ll. 2–4).
421. *What do ye lack*] see l. 93, note.
423.1. *for*] disguised as.   430. *for me*] at that price (Price).
433. *clap hands*] shake, to close the deal.
438. *keys*] to his strong box.

First have I caught him in a bond for two hundred pound,
and . . . my two hundred pound's worth o'cloth again for 440
three-score pound. Admire me, all you students at Inns of
Cozenage.　　　　　　　　　　　　　　　　　　　　　　*Exit.*

Finit Actus Secundus.

[III.i]

Enter Lethe's pander, Hellgill, *the* Country Wench *coming in with a new
fashion gown, dress'd gentlewoman-like, the* Tailor *points it, and* [Mistress
Comings,] *a tirewoman, busy about her head.*

HELLGILL.

You talk of an alteration; here's the thing itself. What base
birth does not raiment make glorious? And what glorious
births do not rags make infamous? Why should not a woman
confess what she is now, since the finest are but deluding
shadows, begot between tirewomen and tailors? For　　　5
instance, behold their parents.

MISTRESS COMINGS.

Say what you will, this wire becomes you best. —How say
you, tailor?

TAILOR.

I promise you 'tis a wire would draw me from my work seven
days a week.　　　　　　　　　　　　　　　　　　　　　　10

---

441. of] *Q1 (cor.), Q2;* for *Q1
(uncor.).*
442.1. *Finit] Q1 (cor.), Q2; Finis
Q1 (uncor.).*

III.i] *Incipit Actus Tertius Q1–2.*
0.2–0.3. Mistress Comings] *Q2; not
in Q1.*
0.3. tirewoman] *Q2;* Tyrewomen
Q1.

440.] Something has dropped out. Price suggests "then recovered." It
might be a phrase like "now have I," which the compositor could overlook
since it repeats the words directly above it in the type.

442. *Cozenage*] cheating, punning on the Inns of Court (l. 88).

44? 1. *Finit*] ends.

[III.i]

0.2. *points it*] ties the laces (Bullen).

0.3. *tirewoman*] see Dramatis Personae, l. 20, note.

6. *behold*] indicating Mistress Comings and the Tailor; perhaps they
(and the Wench) do not enter until this point. His speech is a kind of
prologue to the scene, which, as Dyce notes, is located in the Wench's
lodging.

7. *wire*] frame for her headdress (see I.ii.13–14, note).

COUNTRY WENCH.

Why, do you work o'Sundays, tailor?

TAILOR.

Hardest of all o'Sundays, because we are most forbidden.

COUNTRY WENCH.

Troth, and so do most of us women; the better day the
better deed, we think.

MISTRESS COMINGS.

Excellent, exceeding, i'faith. A narrow-ear'd wire sets out   15
a cheek so fat and so full, and if you be rul'd by me, you
shall wear your hair still like a mock-face behind; 'tis such
an Italian world, many men know not before from behind.

TAILOR.

How like you the sitting of this gown now, Mistress
Comings?   20

MISTRESS COMINGS.

It sits at marvelous good ease and comely discretion.

HELLGILL.

Who would think now this fine sophisticated squall came out
of the bosom of a barn, and the loins of a hay-tosser?

COUNTRY WENCH.

Out, you saucy, pestiferous pander! I scorn that, i'faith.

HELLGILL.

Excellent, already the true phrase and style of a strumpet.   25
Stay, a little more of the red, and then I take my leave of
your cheek for four and twenty hours. —Do you not think it
impossible that her own father should know her now, if he
saw her?

COUNTRY WENCH.

Why, I think no less. How can he know me, when I scarce   30
know myself?

11. S.P.] *Dyce; Curt[ezan] Q1–2*
throughout scene.

___

17. *still*] always.

17. *mock-face*] arrangement of the hair, apparently rudely resembling a
face (Sampson).

18. *Italian*] Jests on their supposed predilection for this sexual perversion
are common. Cf. Middleton's *A Mad World, My Masters*, III.iii.59, and
A Game at Chess, I.i.306; and Dekker's *1 Honest Whore*, II.i.355.

22. *squall*] see I.ii.4, note.

24. *pestiferous*] plague-bearing.   26. *red*] rouge.

HELLGILL.

   'Tis right.

COUNTRY WENCH.

   But so well you lay wait for a man for me!

HELLGILL.

   I protest I have bestowed much labor about it; and in fit
time, good news, I hope.   35

   Enter [a Servant] *bringing in her* Father *in disguise to serve her.*

SERVANT.

   I've found one yet at last, in whose preferment I hope to
reap credit.

COUNTRY WENCH.

   Is that the fellow?

SERVANT.

   Lady, it is.

COUNTRY WENCH.

   Art thou willing to serve me, fellow?   40

FATHER.

   So please you, he that has not the heart to serve such a
mistress as your beautiful self, deserves to be honored for a
fool, or knighted for a coward.

COUNTRY WENCH.

   There's too many of them already.

FATHER.

   'Twere sin then to raise the number.   45

COUNTRY WENCH.

   Well, we'll try both our likings for a month, and then either
proceed or let fall the suit.

35.1. *a* Servant] *Sampson; one Q 1–2.*	*line in Q 1–2.*
36. S.P.] *Dyce;* 1 *Q 1–2.*	39. S.P.] *Dyce;* 1 *Q 1–2.*
36. I've . . . whose] *Dyce; separate*	44. too] *Q 2;* to *Q 1.*

---

   33. *so well*] ironical.

   33. *lay . . . man*] search out a servant.

   35.1. *Servant*] probably Hellgill's (so Dyce in his S.D.).

   44.] see I.i.180, note.

   46. *try . . . likings*] see how we like each other.

   47. *proceed . . . suit*] The legal metaphor continues through the next
two speeches.

FATHER.

Be it as you have spoke, but 'tis my hope
A longer Term.

COUNTRY WENCH.

No, truly, our Term ends once a month; we should get more   50
than the lawyers, for they have but four Terms a year, and
we have twelve, and that makes 'em run so fast to us in the
vacation.

FATHER [*aside*].

A mistress of a choice beauty! Amongst such imperfect
creatures I ha' not seen a perfecter; I should have reckoned   55
the fortunes of my daughter amongst the happiest, had
she lighted into such a service, whereas now I rest doubtful
whom or where she serves.

COUNTRY WENCH [*giving money*].

There's for your bodily advice, Tailor; and there's for
your head-counsel; and I discharge you both till tomorrow   60
morning again.

TAILOR.

At which time our neatest attendance.

MISTRESS COMINGS.

I pray, have an especial care, howsoever you stand or lie,
that nothing fall upon your hair to batter your wire.

                    Exeunt [Tailor *and* Mistress Comings].

COUNTRY WENCH.

I warrant you for that. —Which gown becomes me best now,   65
the purple satin or this?

HELLGILL.

If my opinion might rule over you—

                    Enter Lethe *with* Rearage *and* Salewood.

LETHE.

Come, gallants, I'll bring you to a beauty shall strike your

48. 'tis] *Q1;* its *Q2.*   (*uncor.*).
54. S.D.] *Dyce.*   59. S.D.] *Dyce* (*subs.*).
54. of] *Q1* (*cor.*), *Q2;* of of *Q1*   63. S.P.] *Q2* (*Com*)*; Coin Q1.*

48. *'tis my hope*] I hope for.
51. *four Terms*] see Induction, l. 29.1, note.
54–55. *imperfect creatures*] all women (Price).

eyes into your hearts; what you see you shall desire, yet
never enjoy.   70

REARAGE.

And that's a villainous torment.

SALEWOOD.

And is she but your underput, Master Lethe?

LETHE.

No more, of my credit; and a gentlewoman of a great house,
noble parentage, unmatchable education, my plain pung. I
may grace her with the name of a courtesan, a backslider, a   75
prostitution, or such a toy; but when all comes to all, 'tis
but a plain pung. Look you, gentlemen, that's she; behold
her!

COUNTRY WENCH.

Oh, my beloved strayer! I consume in thy absence.

LETHE.

La, you now! You shall not say I'll be proud to you, gentle-   80
men; I give you leave to salute her. —[Aside.] I'm afraid
of nothing now, but that she'll utterly disgrace 'em, turn
tail to 'em, and place their kisses behind her. No, by my
faith, she deceives me; by my troth, sh'as kiss'd 'em both
with her lips. I thank you for that music, masters. 'Slid,   85
they both court her at once, and see, if she ha' not the wit
to stand still and let 'em! I think if two men were brew'd
into one, there is that woman would drink 'em up both.

REARAGE [to her].

A coxcomb! He a courtier?

COUNTRY WENCH.

He says he has a place there.   90

76. to] *Q2;* ro *Q1.*   89. S.D.] *Sampson* (subs.).
81. S.D.] *Dyce.*

---

72. *underput*] harlot (Sampson).
74. *pung*] variant of "punk," a prostitute (Bullen).
76. *toy*] whim, fancy (Dyce).
76. *when all comes to all*] when all's said and done.
79. *consume*] pine away.   81. *salute*] see II.iii.397, note.
85. *music*] the "smack" of the kisses.
89. *coxcomb*] conceited fool, referring to Lethe. They "court" her at
some distance from him (cf. l. 95).
90. *place there*] position at Court.

SALEWOOD.

So has the fool, a better place than he, and can come where
he dare not show his head.

LETHE.

Nay, hear you me, gentlemen—

SALEWOOD.

I protest you were the last man we spoke on. We're a little
busy yet; pray, stay there awhile; we'll come to you   95
presently.

LETHE [aside].

This is good, i'faith; endure this, and be a slave forever!
Since you neither savor of good breeding nor bringing up,
I'll slice your hamstrings, but I'll make you show mannerly.
—Pox on you, leave courting! I ha' not the heart to hurt   100
an Englishman, i'faith, or else—

SALEWOOD.

What else?

LETHE.

Prithee, let's be merry; nothing else. —Here, fetch some
wine.

COUNTRY WENCH.

Let my servant go for't.   105

LETHE.

Yours? Which is he?

FATHER.

This, sir.—
[Aside.] But I scarce like my mistress now; the loins
Can ne'er be safe where the flies be so busy.

97. S.D.] *Dyce.*   108. S.D.] *Dyce.*
103. S.P.] *Q 1 (Leth); Seth Q 2.*   108–109.] *this edn.; prose in Q 1–2.*
107. S.P.] *Dyce; Sho Q 1–2.*

---

91. *fool*] the king's professional jester.
91. *come*] into the more exalted Court circles.
98–99. *Since . . . mannerly*] He mutters to himself the threats he dare not
make openly to Rearage and Salewood.
100. *leave*] leave off, stop.
100–101. *I . . . Englishman*] Price and Maxwell see a reference to Lethe's
Scottish origin, although this could be spoken by an Englishman ("I won't
fight a fellow countryman").
103. *Here*] probably to Hellgill's Servant (see l. 35.1, note).
109. *flies*] cf. I.ii.48.

Wit, by experience bought, foils wit at school;   110
Who proves a deeper knave than a spent fool?—
I am gone for your worship's wine, sir.   [*Exit.*]

HELLGILL [*taking* Lethe *aside*].

Sir, you put up too much indignity; bring company to cut
your own throat. The fire is not yet so hot, that you need
two screens before it; 'tis but new kindled yet. If 'twere risse   115
to a flame, I could not blame you then to put others before
you; but, alas, all the heat yet is comfortable; a cherisher,
not a defacer.

LETHE.

Prithee, let 'em alone; they'll be asham'd on't anon, I trow,
if they have any grace in 'em.   120

HELLGILL [*aside*].

I'd fain have him quarrel, fight, and be assuredly kill'd,
that I might beg his place, for there's ne'er a one void yet.

[*Exit.*]

Enter Shortyard, [*alias* Blastfield,] *with* Easy.

COUNTRY WENCH.

You'll make him mad anon.

SALEWOOD.

'Tis to that end.

SHORTYARD.

Yet at last Master Quomodo is as firm as his promise.   125

112. S.D.] *Dyce.*   121. S.D.] *Dyce.*
113. S.D.] *this edn.*   122.1.] *Price.*
115. risse] *Q 1;* rissen *Q 2.*

110–111.] "This inexperienced wench studying worldly ways is no
match for the *roués* with whom she is tilting," according to Price; but this
may be simply a general observation based on the Father's own youth
(see ll. 270–271 and II.ii.20–30, and cf. IV.iii.17). The application of
l. 111 is not clear.

113. *put up*] put up with (see II.i.3, note).
114. *fire*] of her passion.
115. *two screens*] Rearage and Salewood.   115. *risse*] risen.
119. *trow*] think, believe.   122. *place*] see l. 90.
122.1.] This is an appropriate exit speech, as Price notes, and it seems
better to have him leave here (perhaps with his Servant) than to remain on
stage, silent, until a general exit at l. 254.1 (as in Dyce *seq.*).
123. *him*] Lethe.   124.] That's our purpose.
125. *promise*] see II.iii.119–121.

EASY.

Did I not tell you still he would?

SHORTYARD.

Let me see, I am seven hundred pound in bond now to the
rascal.

EASY.

Nay, y'are no less, Master Blastfield, look to't. By my
troth, I must needs confess, sir, you ha' been uncommonly 130
kind to me since I ha' been in town; but Master Alsup
shall know on't.

SHORTYARD.

That's my ambition, sir.

EASY.   I beseech you, sir—
Stay, this is Lethe's haunt; see, we have catch'd him.

LETHE.

Master Blastfield and Master Easy, y'are kind   135
Gentlemen both.

SHORTYARD.

Is that the beauty you fam'd so?

LETHE.

The same.

SHORTYARD.

Who be those so industrious about her?

LETHE.

Rearage and Salewood. I'll tell you the unmannerliest trick 140
of 'em, that ever you heard in your life.

SHORTYARD.

Prithee, what's that?

LETHE.

I invited 'em hither to look upon her, brought 'em along
with me, gave 'em leave to salute her in kindness; what do
they but most saucily fall in love with her, very impudently 145
court her for themselves, and, like two crafty attorneys,
finding a hole in my lease, go about to defeat me of my right?

140. I'll] *Q2;* lle *Q1.*

---

134. *haunt*] where he spends his time (cf. I.i.114).
137. *fam'd*] made famous (by his boasting).
147. *hole*] loophole.
147. *right*] title to her.

SHORTYARD.

Ha' they so little conscience?

LETHE.

The most uncivil'st part that you have seen! I know they'll
be sorry for't when they have done, for there's no man but 150
gives a sigh after his sin of women; I know it by myself.

SHORTYARD [to them].

You parcel of a rude, saucy, and unmannerly nation—

LETHE [aside].

One good thing in him, he'll tell 'em on't roundly.

SHORTYARD.

Cannot a gentleman purchase a little fire to thaw his
appetite by, but must you, that have been daily sing'd in the 155
flame, be as greedy to beguile him on't? How can it appear
in you but maliciously, and that you go about to engross hell
to yourselves? Heaven forbid, that you should not suffer a
stranger to come in; the devil himself is not so unmannerly.
I do not think but some of them rather will be wise enough 160
to beg offices there before you, and keep you out; marry,
all the spite will be, they cannot sell 'em again.

EASY.

Come, are you not to blame? Not to give place—
To us, I mean.

LETHE.   A worse and worse disgrace!

COUNTRY WENCH.

Nay, gentlemen, you wrong us both then. Stand from me; I 165

152. S.D.] this edn.   164. and worse] Dyce; and a
153. S.D.] Dyce.   worse Q1–2.
163. to blame] Q1; too blame Q2.

---

149. part] role (Price).

151. gives . . . women] repents his sexual sins.

152. S.D.] Maxwell says this is addressed to Lethe and the Scots; but
in l. 152 Shortyard is pretending to attack Rearage and Salewood (the
parcel: a small group), and so the English (the nation), to set up his attack
on the Scots in his next speech.

154. fire] cf. l. 114.   157. engross] monopolize.

159. stranger] foreigner, here a Scotsman, Lethe.

160. them] the strangers (Scots); a thrust at their filling the offices (l. 161)
at Court under James I (Eccles).

162. 'em] offices, which were often sold at this time.

164. To us] Here Easy and Shortyard move in to court her.

165. us] Lethe and her (Price).

protest I'll draw my silver bodkin upon you.

SHORTYARD.

Clubs, clubs! Gentlemen, stand upon your guard.

COUNTRY WENCH.

A gentlewoman must swagger a little now and then, I perceive; there would be no civility in her chamber else.
Though it be my hard fortune to have my keeper there a   170
coward, the thing that's kept is a gentlewoman born.

SHORTYARD.

And, to conclude, a coward, infallible of your side; why do
you think, i'faith, I took you to be a coward? Do I think
you'll turn your back to any man living? You'll be whip'd
first.   175

EASY.

And then indeed she turns her back to some man living.

SHORTYARD.

But that man shows himself a knave, for he dares not show
his own face when he does it; for some of the Common
Council in Henry the Eight's days thought it modesty at that
time that one vizard should look upon another.   180

EASY.

'Twas honestly considered of 'em, i'faith.

Enter Mother Gruel.

SHORTYARD.

How now? What piece of stuff comes here?

---

166. *bodkin*] long hairpin.

167. *Clubs*] rallying cry used to call out the London apprentices during a
fight (Dyce).

172. *infallible . . . side*] Sampson glosses: "infallibly by your reasoning,"
which does not help much. The text may be corrupt.

172–173. *why . . . think*] what makes you think, not why I took (or *why*
may be an interjection); the point of his joke is that she is not a coward,
since she will take on any man.

174. *whip'd*] the usual punishment for prostitutes.

175. *first*] rather than turn your back.

177–178. *he . . . face*] the public whipping officer wore a mask (*vizard*,
l. 180) (Sampson).

178–179. *Common Council*] governing body of London.

179. *Henry the Eight's days*] 1509–1547. Sampson sees an allusion to the
prohibition of masks for mummings in 1511.

182. *piece of stuff*] term of humorous contempt, harlot (Sampson).

LETHE [*aside*].

Now, some good news yet to recover my repute, and grace
me in this company. —Gentlemen, are we friends among
ourselves?   185

SHORTYARD.

United.

[*Enter* Father *with wine.*]

LETHE.

Then here comes Rhenish to confirm our amity.—
Wagtail, salute them all, they are friends.

COUNTRY WENCH.

Then, saving my quarrel, to you all.

SHORTYARD.

To's all.   190

COUNTRY WENCH.

Now beshrow your hearts, and you do not.

SHORTYARD.

To sweet Master Lethe.

LETHE.

Let it flow this way, dear Master Blastfield. —Gentlemen,
to you all.

SHORTYARD.

This Rhenish wine is like the scouring-stick to a gun, it 195
makes the barrel clear; it has an excellent virtue, it keeps
all the sinks in man and woman's body sweet in June and
July; and, to say truth, if ditches were not cast once a year,
and drabs once a month, there would be no abiding i'th'
city.   200

183. S.D.] *Dyce.*   186.1.] *Dyce.*

---

187. *Rhenish*] Rhine wine.
188. *Wagtail*] harlot (Sampson), here used familiarly.
189. *saving*] except for, without　　　up.
191. *beshrow*] beshrew.
191. *do not*] drink to that toast (*sa　　e*, l. 188).
196. *barrel*] body (Sampson).
197. *sinks*] excretory organs.
198. *ditches . . . year*] see I.i.64, note.
199. *drabs . . . month*] perhaps referring to the terms for "keeping"
mistresses (cf. l. 50), or to a monthly "physic."

LETHE.

Gentlemen, I'll make you privy to a letter I sent.

SHORTYARD.

A letter comes well after privy; it makes amends.

LETHE.

There's one Quomodo a draper's daughter in town,
Whom for her happy portion I wealthily affect.

REARAGE.

And not for love?—   205
[*To* Salewood.] This makes for me, his rival; bear witness.

LETHE.

The father does elect me for the man,
The daughter says the same.

SHORTYARD.   Are you not well?

LETHE.

Yes, all but for the mother; she's my sickness.

SHORTYARD.

By'rlady, and the mother is a pestilent, willful, troublesome 210
sickness, I can tell you, if she light upon you handsomely.

LETHE.

I find it so; she for a stranger pleads,
Whose name I ha' not learn'd.

REARAGE [*to* Salewood].   And e'en now he call'd me by it.

LETHE.

Now, as my letter told her, since only her consent kept
aloof off, what might I think on't but that she merely 215
doted upon me herself?

201. Gentlemen] *Q1;* Gentleman *Q2.*
203–204.] *Price conj.; prose* (?) *in Q1–2.*
205–206.] *Dyce* (*subs.*); *prose in Q1–2.*
206. S.D.] *Dyce.*
213. S.D.] *Price.*
215. off] *Dyce;* of *Q1–2.*
216. doted] *Q2* (doated); dooted *Q1.*

---

201. *privy*] let in on the secret (.i.32); but Shortyard takes it in the sense of "outhouse."
204. *portion*] dowry.
206. *makes for me*] is to my advantage (Price). He and Salewood converse out of Lethe's hearing (cf. ll. 213, 218).
208. *well*] well off (Price).
210. *By'rlady*] by our Lady.
210. *the mother*] a name for hysteria.

SHORTYARD.

Very assuredly.

SALEWOOD [*to* Rearage].

This makes still for you.

SHORTYARD.

Did you let it go so, i'faith?

LETHE.

You may believe it, sir. —Now, what says her answer?   220

SHORTYARD.

Ay, her answer.

MOTHER GRUEL.

She says you're a base, proud knave, and like your worship.

LETHE.

How?

SHORTYARD.

Nay, hear out her answer, or there's no goodness in you.

MOTHER GRUEL.

You ha' forgot, she says, in what pickle your worship came   225
up, and brought two of your friends to give their words for
a suit of green kersey.

LETHE.

Drudge, peace, or—

SHORTYARD.

Show yourself a gentleman; she had the patience to read
your letter, which was as bad as this can be; what will she   230
think on't? Not hear her answer! —Speak, good his drudge.

MOTHER GRUEL.

And as for her daughter, she hopes she'll be rul'd by her
in time, and not be carried away with a cast of manchets, a
bottle of wine, and a custard, which once made her daughter
sick, because you came by it with a bad conscience.   235

LETHE.

Gentlemen, I'm all in a sweat.

218. S.D.] *Price.*   232. S.P.] *Q2 (Gruil); Guil Q1.*
224. Nay] *Q1; May Q2.*

_____

219. *let it go so*] send it with such a message (Price).
225. *pickle*] sorry plight.
229. *she*] Thomasine.

SHORTYARD.

That's very wholesome for your body; nay, you must keep in
your arms.

MOTHER GRUEL.

Then she demanded of me whether I was your worship's
aunt or no.   240

LETHE.

Out, out, out!

MOTHER GRUEL.

Alas, said I, I am a poor drudge of his. —Faith, and thou
wert his mother, quoth she, he'd make thee his drudge, I
warrant him. —Marry, out upon him, quoth I, an't like
your worship.   245

LETHE.

Horror, horror! I'm smother'd; let me go, torment me not.

                                                        Exit.

SHORTYARD.

And you love me, let's follow him, gentlemen.

REARAGE. SALEWOOD.

Agreed.   *Exeunt.*

SHORTYARD.

I count a hundred pound well spent to pursue a good jest,
Master Easy.   250

EASY.

By my troth, I begin to bear that mind too.

SHORTYARD.

Well said, i'faith; hang money! Good jests are worth silver
at all times.

EASY.

They're worth gold, Master Blastfield.

                Exeunt [all except Country Wench *and her* Father].

248. S.P.] *Dyce; All Q1–2.*   254.1. *all . . . Father] Dyce.*

---

238. *arms*] apparently Lethe made a threatening gesture to her, as
Price notes (cf. l. 228).

240. *aunt*] see II.iii.24, note.

248. S.P.] Dyce's emendation seems justified, since they are the only
ones who could follow Lethe here.

251. *bear that mind*] hold that opinion.

254.1.] This would include Mother Gruel (and see l. 122.1, note).

COUNTRY WENCH.

> Do you deceive me so? Are you toward marriage, i'faith,   255
> Master Lethe? It shall go hard but I'll forbid the banes;
> I'll send a messenger into your bones, another into your
> purse, but I'll do't.   *Exit.*

FATHER.

> Thou fair and wicked creature, steep'd in art,
> Beauteous and fresh, the soul the foulest part!   260
> A common filth is like a house possess'd,
> Where, if not spoil'd, you'll come out fray'd at least.
> This service likes not me; though I rest poor,
> I hate the basest use, to screen a whore.
> The human stroke ne'er made him; he that can   265
> Be bawd to woman never leapt from man;
> Some monster won his mother.
> I wish'd my poor child hither, doubled wrong!
> A month and such a mistress were too long;
> Yet here awhile in others' lives I'll see   270
> How former follies did appear in me.   *Exit.*

256. Lethe] *Q1;* Lethes *Q2.*   'fraid *Dyce seq.*
262. fray'd] *this edn.;* fraide *Q1–2;*   268. hither] *Dyce;* hether *Q1–2.*

---

255. *toward*] thinking of (Sampson), approaching.
256. *banes*] banns, required public notice of an intended marriage to bring to light any impediments.
257–258. *send . . . purse*] give you syphilis (see II.i.145, note) and poverty (Price, who notes the pun on *banes* and *bones*).
259. *art*] artfulness (Price), artifice.
261. *common filth*] prostitute.
261. *possess'd*] by devils, haunted. The quarto spelling, *possest,* indicates the rhyme.
262. *fray'd*] Dyce's *'fraid* ("afraid") fits *possess'd* (l. 261), but seems less likely after *spoil'd,* as describing the result of contact with a prostitute. But see III.iii.54, IV.i.101.
263. *likes*] pleases (Dyce).
264. *use*] practice, of a *bawd,* l. 266 (Price).
265. *stroke*] in intercourse.
266. *leapt*] was born, sprang.

[III.ii]   *Enter* Easy *with Shortyard's* Boy.

EASY.

  Boy!

BOY.

  Anon, sir.

EASY.

  Where left you Master Blastfield, your master, say you?

BOY.

  An hour since I left him in Paul's, sir. —[*Aside.*] But you'll
  not find him the same man again, next time you meet him.   5

EASY.

  Methinks I have no being without his company; 'tis so full
  of kindness and delight, I hold him to be the only companion
  in earth.

BOY [*aside*].

  Ay, as companions go nowadays, that help to spend a man's
  money.   10

EASY.

  So full of nimble wit, various discourse, pregnant apprehen-
  sion, and uncommon entertainment! He might keep company with any lord for his grace.

BOY [*aside*].

  Ay, with any lord that were past it.

EASY.

  And such a good, free-hearted, honest, affable kind of   15
  gentleman. Come, boy, a heaviness will possess me till I see
  him.   *Exit.*

BOY.

  But you'll find yourself heavier then, by a seven hundred
  pound weight. Alas, poor birds that cannot keep the sweet
  country, where they fly at pleasure, but must needs come to 20

III.ii] *Dyce; no scene division in Q 1–2.*   9. S.D.] *Dyce.*
3. S.P.] *Q 1 (Eas); Fals Q 2.*   14. S.D.] *Dyce.*
4. S.D.] *Dyce.*

---

  4. *Paul's*] see I.i.134, note.
  14. *past it*] past grace, a reprobate (Price); cf. II.iii.410–412.
  16. *heaviness*] sadness; but the Boy takes it literally, in a pun on the two
meanings of *pound* (l. 19).

London to have their wings clip'd, and are fain to go
hopping home again.   *Exit.*

[III.iii]
Enter Shortyard *and* Falselight, *like a Sergeant and a Yeoman, to arrest*
Easy.

SHORTYARD.

So, no man is so impudent to deny that. Spirits can change
their shapes, and soonest of all into sergeants, because
they are cousin-germans to spirits; for there's but two
kind of arrests till doomsday: the devil for the soul, the
sergeant for the body; but afterward the devil arrests body   5
and soul, sergeant and all, if they be knaves still and deserve
it. Now, my Yeoman Falselight—

FALSELIGHT.

I attend you, good Sergeant Shortyard.

SHORTYARD.

No more Master Blastfield now. Poor Easy, hardly beset!

FALSELIGHT.

But how if he should go to prison? We're in a mad state   10
then, being not sergeants.

SHORTYARD.

Never let it come near thy belief that he'll take prison, or
stand out in law, knowing the debt to be due, but still
expect the presence of Master Blastfield, kind Master Blastfield, worshipful Master Blastfield, and at the last—   15

III.iii] *Dyce; no scene division in*   1. So ... that] *Dyce; separate line in*
Q *1–2.*   Q *1–2.*

---

21. *wings clip'd*] cf. II.iii.344.
21. *fain*] obliged.
[III.iii]
0.1. *Sergeant*] sheriff's officer who made arrests; he was assisted by a
Yeoman (see l. 8).
1. *Spirits*] see Introduction, p. xvii.
3. *cousin-germans*] first cousins.
9. *beset*] besieged, assailed (Price).
10. *mad state*] foolish, dangerous position (Sampson).
12. *take prison*] accept imprisonment.
13. *stand out in law*] challenge the suit in court.

BOY [*within*].

> Master Shortyard, Master Falselight!

SHORTYARD.

> The boy, a warning-piece! See where he comes.

Enter Easy *with the* Boy.

EASY.

> Is not in Paul's.

BOY.

> He is not far off, sure, sir.

EASY.

> When was his hour, sayst thou?   20

BOY.

> Two, sir.

EASY.

> Why, two has struck.

BOY.

> No, sir, they are now a-striking.

SHORTYARD.

> Master Richard Easy of Essex, we arrest you.

EASY.

> Hah?   25

BOY.

> Alas, a surgeon! He's hurt i'th' shoulder.   [*Exit.*]

SHORTYARD.

> Deliver your weapons quietly, sir.

EASY.

> Why, what's the matter?

SHORTYARD.

> Y'are arrested at the suit of Master Quomodo.

16. S.D.] *Dyce.*   26. S.D.] *Dyce.*

---

16. S.D.] He has run ahead of Easy, while pretending to look for Blast-field, in order to warn them (Price).

17. *warning-piece*] signal gun (Sampson).

20. *his hour*] when Blastfield was due at St. Paul's.

23. *a-striking*] clapping him on the shoulder (l. 26) to make the arrest (Sampson).

27. *weapons*] his sword, and perhaps a dagger.

EASY.

> Master Quomodo?   30

SHORTYARD.

> How strange you make it! You're a landed gentleman, sir, I
> know; 'tis but a trifle, a bond of seven hundred pound.

EASY.

> La, I knew you had mistook; you should arrest
> One Master Blastfield, 'tis his bond, his debt.

SHORTYARD.

> Is not your name there?   35

EASY.

> True, for fashion's sake.

SHORTYARD.

> Why, and 'tis for fashion's sake that we arrest you.

EASY.

> Nay, and it be no more, I yield to that. I know Master
> Blastfield will see me take no injury as long as I'm in town,
> for Master Alsup's sake.   40

SHORTYARD.

> Who's that, sir?

EASY.

> An honest gentleman in Essex.

SHORTYARD.

> Oh, in Essex! I thought you had been in London, where now
> your business lies; honesty from Essex will be a great while
> a-coming, sir; you should look out an honest pair of citizens.   45

EASY.

> Alas, sir, I know not where to find 'em.

SHORTYARD.

> No? There's enow in town.

EASY.

> I know not one, by my troth; I am a mere stranger for these
> parts; Master Quomodo is all, and the honestest, that I
> know.   50

32. know; 'tis] *Dyce;* knew tis *Q1;*   33. knew] *Dyce;* knowe *Q1–2.*
know tis *Q2.*

31–32. *I know*] may belong to the next clause, as Price believes (see
textual note).
43. *been in*] been talking about.
45. *citizens*] for bail (see III.iv.89).

SHORTYARD.

To him, then, let's set forward. —Yeoman Spiderman, cast
an eye about for Master Blastfield.

EASY.

Boy— Alas, the poor boy was frighted away at first.

SHORTYARD.

Can you blame him, sir? We that daily fray away knights,
may fright away boys, I hope.   *Exeunt.*   55

[III.iv]

    Enter Quomodo *with the* Boy, [Thomasine *watching above*].

QUOMODO.

Hah! Have they him, sayst thou?

BOY.   As sure as—

QUOMODO.

The land's mine; that's sure enough, boy.
Let me advance thee, knave, and give thee a kiss;
My plot's so firm, I dare it now to miss.
Now shall I be divulg'd a landed man   5
Throughout the Livery; one points, another whispers,
A third frets inwardly, let him fret and hang!
Especially his envy I shall have
That would be fain, yet cannot be, a knave,
Like an old lecher, girt in a fur'd gown,   10
Whose mind stands stiff, but his performance down.
Now come my golden days in.
—Whither is the worshipful Master Quomodo and his

III.iv] *Dyce; no scene division in*   1. they] *Q1; not in Q2.*
Q1–2.   10. lecher] *Dyce;* leather *Q1–2.*
0.1. Thomasine . . . *above*] *Dyce.*   10. a] *Q2; not in Q1.*

---

54. *fray*] make afraid, frighten.
[III.iv]
    0.1.] The scene is located in Quomodo's shop (Dyce); Thomasine
watches, unseen, from the "gallery" (as in II.iii), presumably from the
start, but does not speak until l. 148.
    3. *advance*] raise, promote.
    6. *Livery*] see II.iii.415, note.
    9. *fain*] gladly.
    10. *girt*] girded, wrapped.
    11. *stands . . . down*] cf. II.iii.66–67.

fair bedfellow rid forth? —To his land in Essex! —Whence
comes those goodly load of logs? —From his land in Essex!   15
—Where grows this pleasant fruit? says one citizen's wife
in the Row. —At Master Quomodo's orchard in Essex.
—Oh, oh, does it so? I thank you for that good news, i'faith.

BOY.

Here they come with him, sir.   [*Exit.*]

QUOMODO.

Grant me patience in my joys, that, being so great, I run   20
not mad with 'em.

[*Enter* Shortyard *and* Falselight, *disguised as a Sergeant and a Yeoman,
bringing in* Easy.]

SHORTYARD.

Bless Master Quomodo!

QUOMODO.

How now, sergeants? Who ha' you brought me here?
—Master Easy!

EASY.

Why, la you now, sergeants, did I not tell you you mistook?   25

QUOMODO.

Did you not hear me say, I had rather ha' had Master
Blastfield, the more sufficient man a great deal?

SHORTYARD.

Very true, sir, but this gentleman lighting into our hands
first—

QUOMODO.

Why, did you so, sir?   30

SHORTYARD.

We thought good to make use of that opportunity, and hold
him fast.

---

19. S.D.] *Dyce.*   26. ha' had] *Q1;* had *Q2.*
21.1–2.] *Dyce (subs.).*   30. Why,] *this edn.;* Why *Q1–2.*

---

17. *Row*] probably Goldsmith's Row in Cheapside (Dyce), a street of
wealthy shops and homes.

27. *sufficient*] financially (Sampson; cf. l. 58).

30.] perhaps to Shortyard (Price, and apparently Dyce *seq.*), but more
likely to Easy, for he *did* something ("lighted"). Hence the comma after
Why, since he would not be asked to explain his doing so.

QUOMODO.

You did well in that, I must needs say, for your own securi-
ties. But 'twas not my mind, Master Easy, to have you first,
you must needs think so.   35

EASY.

I dare swear that, Master Quomodo.

QUOMODO.

But since you are come to me, I have no reason to refuse you;
I should show little manners in that, sir.

EASY.

But I hope you spake not in that sense, sir, to impose the
bond upon me?   40

QUOMODO.

By my troth, that's my meaning, sir; you shall find me an
honest man, you see I mean what I say. Is not the day past,
the money untender'd? You'd ha' me live uprightly, Master
Easy?

EASY.

Why, sir, you know Master Blastfield is the man.   45

QUOMODO.

Why, sir, I know Master Blastfield is the man; but is he any
more than one man? Two enter'd into bond to me, or I'm
foully cozen'd.

EASY.

You know my entrance was but for fashion sake.

QUOMODO.

Why, I'll agree to you; you'll grant 'tis the fashion like-   50
wise, when the bond's due, to have the money paid again.

SHORTYARD.

So we told him, sir, and that it lay in your worship's
courtesy to arrest which you please.

QUOMODO.

Marry, does it, sir; these fellows know the law. Beside, you
offer'd yourself into bond to me, you know, when I had no   55
stomach to you; now beshrew your heart for your labor! I

42. man] *Q1;* men *Q2.*   47. enter'd] *Q1;* enter *Q2.*

43. *untender'd*] unpaid.
53. *courtesy*] indulgence, discretion.
56. *stomach*] inclination (Sampson).

might ha' had a good substantial citizen, that would ha' paid
the sum roundly, although I think you sufficient enough for
seven hundred pound; beside the forfeiture, I would be
loath to disgrace you so much before sergeants.   60

EASY.

If you would ha' the patience, sir, I do not think but Master
Blastfield is at carrier's to receive the money.

QUOMODO.

He will prove the honester man, then, and you the better
discharged. I wonder he should break with me; 'twas never
his practice. You must not be angry with me now, though   65
you were somewhat hot when you enter'd into bond; you
may easily go in angrily, but you cannot come out so.

EASY.

No, the devil's in't for that!

SHORTYARD.

Do you hear, sir? [*Taking him aside.*]   O'my troth, we
pity you; ha' you any store of crowns about you?   70

EASY.

Faith, a poor store, yet they shall be at their service that
will strive to do me good. We were both drunk last night,
and ne'er thought upon the bond.

SHORTYARD.

I must tell you this, you have fell into the hands of a most
merciless devourer, the very gull o'the city; should you   75
offer him money, goods, or lands now, he'd rather have your
body in prison, he's o'such a nature.

EASY.

Prison? W'are undone then!

SHORTYARD.

He's o'such a nature, look! Let him owe any man a spite,

69. S.D.] *this edn.*

---

57. *good*] well-to-do, "sufficient" (Sampson).

58. *roundly*] completely, directly, readily.

62. *carrier's*] Each messenger from the provinces had fixed headquarters
at a London inn, where a man expecting money from the country would
go to receive it (Sampson).

72–73. *We . . . bond*] perhaps an aside (Dyce *seq.*).

75. *gull*] probably gullet, swallower; certainly not "dupe," as in ll.
112–113.

what's his course? He will lend him money today, o'purpose   80
to 'rest him tomorrow.

EASY.

Defend me!

SHORTYARD.

H'as at least sixteen at this instant proceeded in both the
Counters: some bach'lors, some masters, some doctors of
captivity of twenty years' standing; and he desires nothing   85
more than imprisonment.

EASY.

Would Master Blastfield would come away!

SHORTYARD.

Ay, then things would not be as they are. What will you
say to us, if we procure you two substantial subsidy citizens
to bail you, spite on's heart, and set you at liberty to   90
find out Master Blastfield?

EASY.

Sergeant, here, take all! I'll be dear to you, do but perform it.

SHORTYARD [aside].

Much!

FALSELIGHT [aside].

Enough, sweet sergeant, I hope I understand thee.   95

SHORTYARD.

I love to prevent the malice of such a rascal; perhaps you

---

84. bach'lors] *Q2;* batchler *Q1.*   95. S.D.] *Price.*
94. S.D.] *Price.*

---

81. *'rest*] arrest (Price).

82.] an oath; "God," "Heaven," etc., understood.

83. *proceeded*] advancing to a higher degree (in a university). This com-
parison of the *Counters* (debtors' prisons—see II.iii.345) to universities also
occurs in Middleton's *The Phoenix*, IV.iii.16–22, and in Middleton and
Dekker's *The Roaring Girl*, III.iii.88–111, as Dyce notes.

89. *subsidy*] see l. 175, note.

92. *take all*] his *poor store* of crowns (l. 71).

94. *Much*] ironical, contemptuous expression meaning "little" or "none"
(Dyce), referring either to what he will *perform* (ll. 92–93) for Easy, or to
the *crowns* (l. 70) just received from him.

95. S.P.] Bullen (following Dyce conj.) gives the speech to Easy, but
Price shows this is most unlikely. Presumably Falselight is responding to
Shortyard's *Much.*

might find Master Blastfield tonight.

EASY.

Why, we lie together, man, there's the jest on't.

SHORTYARD.

Fie! And you'll seek to secure your bail? Because they will
be two citizens of good account; you must do that for your 100
credit sake.

EASY.

I'll be bound to save them harmless.

SHORTYARD.

A pox on him, you cut his throat then. No words!

EASY.

What's it you require me, Master Quomodo?

QUOMODO.

You know that before this time, I hope, sir: present money, 105
or present imprisonment.

SHORTYARD.

I told you so.

EASY.

We ne'er had money of you.

QUOMODO.

You had commodities, an't please you.

EASY.

Well, may I not crave so much liberty upon my word, to 110
seek out Master Blastfield?

QUOMODO.

Yes, and you would not laugh at me. We are sometimes gulls
to gentlemen, I thank 'em; but gentlemen are never gulls to
us, I commend 'em.

SHORTYARD.

Under your leave, Master Quomodo, the gentleman craves 115
the furtherance of an hour; and it sorts well with our

---

98. *lie together*] cf. II.iii.156.
100. *account*] repute, "substance."
102. *save them harmless*] see they lose nothing by it.
103. *No words*] keep mum (Price).
107.] to Easy, perhaps in an aside (Price).
110. *word*] his "parole" or promise not to escape.
112–114. *We . . . 'em*] cf. I.i.85–89.
116. *sorts*] coincides, fits into.

occasion at this time, having a little urgent business at Guildhall; at which minute we'll return, and see what agreement
is made.

QUOMODO.

Nay, take him along with you, sergeant.   120

EASY [*aside*].

I'm undone then!

SHORTYARD.

He's your prisoner, and being safe in your house at your own
disposing, you cannot deny him such a request; beside, he
hath a little faith in Master Blastfield's coming, sir.

QUOMODO.

Let me not be too long delay'd, I charge you.   125

EASY.

Not an hour, i'faith, sir.

                    Exeunt [Shortyard *and* Falselight].

QUOMODO.

Oh, Master Easy, of all men living I never dreamt you would
ha' done me this injury: make me wound my credit, fail in
my commodities, bring my state into suspicion! For the
breaking of your day to me has broken my day to others.   130

EASY.

You tell me of that still which is no fault of mine, Master
Quomodo.

QUOMODO.

Oh, what's a man but his honesty, Master Easy? And that's
a fault amongst most of us all. Mark but this note; I'll give
you good counsel now. As often as you give your name to a   135
bond, you must think you christen a child, and take the

121. S.D.] *this edn.*   *of Q1.*
127. dreamt] *Q2* (dream't); dream'   129. bring] *Q2;* ring *Q1.*
some copies of Q1; dream *most copies*

117–118. *Guildhall*] City Hall of London.

127. *dreamt*] Q1 has blank spaces here and at ll. 129, 152 (all on F4ᵛ),
where the missing letters presumably dropped out.

129. *state*] financial standing (Sampson).

130. *your day*] when the debt was due.

133. *that's*] breaking one's word (Price).

134. *note*] thing worth noting (Price).

136. *christen*] serve as godparent, taking the spiritual responsibility
(*charge*) for its upbringing.

charge on't, too; for as the one, the bigger it grows, the
more cost it requires, so the other, the longer it lies, the
more charges it puts you to. Only here's the difference: a
child must be broke, and a bond must not; the more you   140
break children, the more you keep 'em under, but the more
you break bonds, the more they'll leap in your face; and
therefore, to conclude, I would never undertake to be gossip
to that bond which I would not see well brought up.

EASY.

Say you so, sir? I'll think upon your counsel hereafter for't.   145

QUOMODO [aside].

Ah, fool, thou shouldst ne'er ha' tasted such wit, but that
I know 'tis too late.

THOMASINE [aside].

The more I grieve.

QUOMODO.

To put all this into the compass of a little hoop ring:
    "Make this account, come better days or worse,   150
        So many bonds abroad, so many boys at nurse."

EASY.

A good medicine for a short memory. But since you have
enter'd so far, whose children are desperate debts, I pray?

QUOMODO.

Faith, they are like the offsprings of stol'n lust, put to the

143. therefore] Q2; therfeore Q1.   152.] Speech Prefix and first word of
146. S.D.] Dyce.   speech (A) omitted in some copies of
148. S.D.] Dyce.   Q1 and in Q2.

---

137. one] the child.
138. lies] remains unpaid.
140. broke] made obedient, "broken in."
143. gossip] godparent.
149.] to make a little rhyme or "posy" of it, such as was often engraved
inside finger rings (Sampson).
151. bonds abroad] debts outstanding.
151. at nurse] see II.iii.166, note.
152. medicine] remedy (Schelling), since the verse form made it easier to
memorize (cf. l. 157).
153. enter'd] into this subject.
153. desperate] defaulted.
154–155. put . . . hospital] abandoned foundlings.

hospital; their fathers are not to be found; they are either 155
too far abroad, or too close within. And thus for your
memory's sake:

> "The desperate debtor hence derives his name,
> One that has neither money, land, nor fame;
> All that he makes prove bastards, and not bands,   160
> But such as yours at first are born to lands."

EASY.

But all that I beget hereafter I'll soon disinherit, Master
Quomodo.

QUOMODO [aside].

In the meantime, here's a shrewd knave will disinherit you.

EASY.

Well, to put you out of all doubt, Master Quomodo, I'll not 165
trust to your courtesy; I ha' sent for bail.

QUOMODO.

How? Y'ave cozen'd me there, i'faith.

EASY.

Since the worst comes to the worst, I have those friends i'th'
city, I hope, that will not suffer me to lie for seven hundred
pound.   170

QUOMODO.

And you told me you had no friends here at all; how should
a man trust you now?

EASY.

That was but to try your courtesy, Master Quomodo.

QUOMODO [aside].

How unconscionably he gulls himself! —They must be

156. too . . . too] *Q1 (cor.), Q2;* to	164. S.D.] *Dyce.*
. . . to *Q1 (uncor.).*	174. S.D.] *Dyce.*
160. bands] *Dyce;* Bonds *Q1–2.*	

155–156. *either . . . within*] either absconded, or imprisoned.

159. *fame*] good reputation, credit.

160. *All*] *debts* (l. 153) understood here, and after *such* (l. 161) (Price).

160. *bands*] variant of *bonds*, emended for the rhyme.

161. *born to lands*] your land "fathers" (guarantees) them, and, perhaps,
will be lost because of them (i.e., your debts will "inherit" your land;
cf. ll. 162–164).

168. *worst . . . worst*] proverbial (Tilley, W 911).

169. *lie*] in custody (Sampson).

174. *unconscionably*] an intensive: egregiously, abominably.

wealthy subsidy-men, sir, at least forty pound i'th' King's   175
Books, I can tell you, that do such a feat for you.

Enter Shortyard *and* Falselight, *like wealthy citizens in satin suits.*

EASY.

Here they come, whatsoe'er they are.

QUOMODO.

By'rlady, alderman's deputies! I am very sorry for you, sir;
I cannot refuse such men.

SHORTYARD.

Are you the gentleman in distress?   180

EASY.

None more than myself, sir.

QUOMODO [*aside*].

He speaks truer than he thinks, for if he knew
The hearts that owe those faces! A dark shop's good
For somewhat.

EASY.

That was all, sir.   185

SHORTYARD.

And that's enough, for by that means you have made yourself liable to the bond, as well as that Basefield.

EASY.

Blastfield, sir.

SHORTYARD.

Oh, cry you mercy, 'tis Blastfield indeed.

EASY.

But, under both your worships' favors, I know where to find   190
him presently.

182. S.D.] *Dyce.*
183–184.] *Price (subs.); prose (?) in Q1–2.*

183. faces] *Q1 (cor.), Q2;* face *Q1 (uncor.).*
189. Blastfield] *Q1 (cor.), Q2;* blastfield *Q1 (uncor.).*

175. *subsidy-men*] men of sufficient wealth to be listed in the tax rolls (*King's Books*) for a special *subsidy* assessment in addition to regular taxes (Sampson).

178. *alderman's deputies*] city officials.

183. *owe*] own; i.e., the real identity behind the disguises.

185.] He has just explained the situation to them.

SHORTYARD.

That's all your refuge.

[*Enter* Boy.]

BOY.

News, good news, Master Easy!

EASY.

What, boy?

BOY.

Master Blastfield, my master, has received a thousand 195
pound, and will be at his lodging at supper.

EASY.

Happy news! Hear you that, Master Quomodo?

QUOMODO.

'Tis enough for you to hear that; y'are the fortunate man,
sir.

EASY.

Not now, I beseech your good worships.   200

SHORTYARD.

Gentleman, what's your tother name?

EASY.

Easy.

SHORTYARD.

Oh, Master Easy. I would we could rather pleasure you
otherwise, Master Easy; you should soon perceive it. I'll
speak a proud word: we have pitied more gentlemen in 205
distress than any two citizens within the freedom. But to be
bail to seven hundred pound action is a matter of shroud
weight.

EASY.

I'll be bound to secure you.

SHORTYARD.

Tut, what's your bond, sir?   210

192.1.] *Dyce.*   207. seven] *Q2;* seanen *Q1.*
201. tother] *Q1;* other *Q2.*

192.] That's your only hope (Price).
200. *Not now*] apparently, "Do not leave me now" (Price).
204. *otherwise*] in some other situation.
206. *freedom*] see I.ii.44, note.
207. *shroud*] shrewd, grievous, serious.

EASY.

>Body, goods, and lands, immediately before Master Quo-
>modo.

SHORTYARD.

>Shall we venture once again, that have been so often undone
>by gentlemen?

FALSELIGHT.

>I have no great stomach to't; it will appear in us more pity   215
>than wisdom.

EASY.

>Why should you say so, sir?

SHORTYARD.

>I like the gentleman's face well; he does not look as if he
>would deceive us.

EASY.

>Oh, not I, sir!   220

SHORTYARD.

>Come, we'll make a desperate voyage once again; we'll try
>his honesty, and take his single bond, of body, goods, and
>lands.

EASY.

>I dearly thank you, sir.

SHORTYARD.

>Master Quomodo!   225

QUOMODO.

>Your worships.

SHORTYARD.

>We have took a course to set your prisoner free.

QUOMODO.

>Your worships are good bail; you content me.

SHORTYARD.

>Come, then, and be a witness to a recullisance.

215. to't] *Q1* (*cor.*); to eate *Q1*   more pittie in vs *Q1* (*uncor.*), *Q2.*
(*uncor.*), *Q2.*   229. and] *Q1* (*cor.*), *Q2; aud Q1*
215. in us more pity] *Q1* (*cor.*);   (*uncor.*).

   211–212.] As security (l. 209), he gives them the right, if he defaults, to
take his property or imprison his *body* (cf. l. 77); this to take precedence
over Quomodo's claim on him.

   229. *recullisance*] recognizance, a document acknowledging a debt and
the security that is forfeit upon default (Price).

QUOMODO.

With all my heart, sir.   230

SHORTYARD.

Master Easy, you must have an especial care now to find out
that Blastfield.

EASY.

I shall have him at my lodging, sir.

SHORTYARD.

The suit will be followed against you else; Master Quomodo
will come upon us, and forsake you.   235

EASY.

I know that, sir.

SHORTYARD.

Well, since I see you have such a good mind to be honest,
I'll leave some greater affairs, and sweat with you to find
him myself.

EASY.

Here, then, my misery ends;   240
A stranger's kindness oft exceeds a friend's.   *Exeunt.*

THOMASINE.

Thou art deceiv'd, thy misery but begins;
"To beguile goodness is the core of sins."
My love is such unto thee, that I die
As often as thou drink'st up injury,   245
Yet have no means to warn thee from't; for "he
That sows in craft does rape in jealousy."   [*Exit above.*]

---

246. "he] *this edn.; quotation marks*   247. rape] *Q1 (cor.);* reape *Q1*
begin l. 247 in Q1–2.   (*uncor.*), *Q2.*

234–235.] Quomodo will demand the £700 from us (as your bailsmen),
and then we must take your forfeiture.

243.] gnomic pointing here and at ll. 246–247 (see I.i.70, note).

245. *drink'st up*] take in, suffer.

247.] Apparently the MS. read *rape*, no doubt with a pun on "reap."
As Eccles suggests, Thomasine seems to mean that the crafty man
(Quomodo) is also very jealous, so that she cannot warn Easy (cf.
IV.i.111); to *rape*, here, would be to seize violently. There may be a causal
connection implied in the imagery of sowing and reaping (cf. IV.i.86–88).

[III.v]   [*Enter* Rearage *and* Salewood.]

REARAGE.

Now the letter's made up and all; it wants but the print of
a seal, and away it goes to Master Quomodo. Andrew Lethe
is well whip'd in't; his name stands in a white sheet here,
and does penance for him.

SALEWOOD.

You have shame enough against him, if that be good.   5

REARAGE.

First, as a contempt of that reverend ceremony he has in
hand, to wit, marriage.

SALEWOOD.

Why do you say, "to wit, marriage," when you know there's
none will marry that's wise?

REARAGE.

Had it not more need, then, to have wit to put to't, if it   10
be grown to a folly?

SALEWOOD.

Y'ave won, I'll give't you.

REARAGE.

'Tis no thanks now. But, as I was saying, as a foul contempt
to that sacred ceremony, he most audaciously keeps a
drab in town; and, to be free from the interruption of blue   15
beadles and other bawdy officers, he most politicly lodges
her in a constable's house.

III.v] *Dyce; no scene division in Q 1–2.*   3. in] *Q 2;* jn *Q 1.*
0.1.] *Dyce.*

---

3. *stands . . . sheet*] required of those doing public *penance.* The custom is
alluded to in Middleton and Rowley's *A Fair Quarrel,* V.i.27–30, as
Sampson notes.
5. *shame*] shameful disclosures.
6–7. *in hand*] in preparation.
12. *I'll give't you*] I give up (Sampson), yield the point.
13. *'Tis . . . now*] thanks for nothing (Sampson).
16. *beadles*] minor officials, who wore *blue* coats (Dyce).
16. *bawdy*] having jurisdiction over sexual offenses.
16. *politicly*] craftily, cunningly.
17. *constable*] parish police officer in charge of the *watch* (l. 19) that
patrolled the streets at night.

SALEWOOD.

That's a pretty point, i'faith.

REARAGE.

And so the watch, that should fetch her out, are her chiefest
guard to keep her in.   20

SALEWOOD.

It must needs be, for look how the constable plays his conscience, the watchmen will follow the suit.

REARAGE.

Why, well then.

Enter Easy *with* Shortyard, *like a citizen.*

EASY.

All night from me? He's hurt, he's made away!

SHORTYARD.

Where shall we seek him now? You lead me fair jaunts, sir.   25

EASY.

Pray, keep a little patience, sir; I shall find him at last,
you shall see.

SHORTYARD.

A citizen of my ease and substance to walk so long afoot!

EASY.

You should ha' had my horse, but that he has eaten out his
head, sir.   30

SHORTYARD.

How? Would you had me hold him by the tail, sir, then?

EASY.

Manners forbid! 'Tis no part of my meaning, sir. Oh, here's
Master Rearage and Master Salewood; now we shall hear of
him presently. —Gentlemen both.

34. Gentlemen] *Q2;* Gntlemen *Q1.*

---

19. *fetch her out*] arrest her.

21. *look how*] however (Price).

22. *follow the suit*] follow his lead, in overlooking the offense (the imagery
is drawn from card-playing).

24. *made away*] murdered (cf. II.iii.418).

25. *jaunts*] fatiguing or troublesome journeys.

29-30. *he . . . head*] He was surrendered to satisfy the accumulated
charges for his board (Sampson; cf. II.iii.285).

SALEWOOD.

    Master Easy, how fare you, sir?   35

EASY.

    Very well in health. Did you see Master Blastfield this morning?

SALEWOOD.

    I was about to move it to you.

REARAGE.

    We were all three in a mind, then.

SALEWOOD.

    I ha' not set eye on him these two days.   40

REARAGE.

    I wonder he keeps so long from us, i'faith.

EASY.

    I begin to be sick.

SALEWOOD.

    Why, what's the matter?

EASY.

    Nothing, in troth, but a great desire I had to have seen him.

REARAGE.

    I wonder you should miss on't lately; you're his bedfellow. 45

EASY.

    I lay alone tonight, i'faith; I do not know how— Oh, here comes Master Lethe; he can dispatch me.

              [*Enter* Lethe.]

    Master Lethe!

LETHE.

    What's your name, sir? Oh, cry you mercy, Master Easy.

EASY.

    When parted you from Master Blastfield, sir?   50

LETHE.

    Blastfield's an ass; I have sought him these two days to beat him.

43. what's] *Q1* (*cor.*), *Q2;* what,s   47.1.] *Dyce.*
Q1 (*uncor.*).   50. Master] *Q2; maistet Q1.*

---

    38. *move . . . you*] ask you that (Sampson).
    39. *in a mind*] of one mind.   46. *tonight*] last night.
    47. *dispatch me*] settle it for me quickly.

EASY.

Yourself all alone, sir?

LETHE.

Ay, and three more. *Exit.*

SHORTYARD [*aside*].

I am glad I am where I am, then; I perceive 'twas time   55
of all hands.

REARAGE [*to* Salewood].

Content, i'faith, let's trace him.

Exeunt after Lethe.

SHORTYARD.

What, have you found him yet? Neither? What's to be done
now? I'll venture my body no further for any gentleman's
pleasure; I know not how soon I may be call'd upon, and   60
now to overheat myself—

EASY.

I'm undone!

SHORTYARD.

This is you that slept with him! You can make fools of us;
but I'll turn you over to Quomodo for't.

EASY.

Good sir—   65

SHORTYARD.

I'll prevent mine own danger.

EASY.

I beseech you, sir—

54. Ay,] *Dyce;* I, *Q1–2.*	57. S.D.] *Price.*
55. S.D.] *Dyce.*	59. venture] *Q2;* venter *Q1.*

54. *Ay*] normally spelled *I* in Q1–2, and so sometimes ambiguous (as
here). As Price notes, the comma suggests that *Ay*, rather than the pronoun,
is intended.

55. *where I am*] i.e., in another disguise.

56. *of all hands*] on all accounts (Price).

57. *Content*] agreed. They have been conversing aside and presumably
intend to find Lethe's latest concealment for the Wench (Price; cf. III.i.206–
218, IV.iii.43–45).

60. *call'd upon*] summoned by death (Sampson, on IV.iii.5).

66. *prevent*] forestall.

66. *danger*] see III.iv.234–235, note.

SHORTYARD.

Though I love gentlemen well, I do not mean to be undone
for 'em.

EASY.

Pray, sir, let me request you, sir; sweet sir, I beseech you,   70
sir—   *Exeunt.*

Music. Finit Actus Tertius.

[IV.i]

Enter Quomodo, *his disguised spirits* [Shortyard *and* Falselight, *like
wealthy citizens*], *after whom* Easy *follows hard.*

SHORTYARD.

Made fools of us! Not to be found!

QUOMODO.

What, what?

EASY.

Do not undo me quite, though, Master Quomodo.

QUOMODO.

Y'are very welcome, Master Easy, I ha' nothing to say to
you; I'll not touch you, you may go when you please. I   5
have good bail here, I thank their worships.

EASY.

What shall I say, or whom shall I beseech?

SHORTYARD.

Gentlemen! 'Slid, they were born to undo us, I think;
but, for my part, I'll make an oath before Master Quomodo
here, ne'er to do gentlemen good while I live.   10

FALSELIGHT.

I'll not be long behind you.

SHORTYARD.

Away! If you had any grace in you, you would be ashamed

71.1. *Finit*] *Q1* (*uncor.*), *Q2; Finis*   IV.i] *Incipit quartus Q1–2.*
Q1 (*cor.*).

71.1. *Music*] played in the intermission between acts.
71.1. *Finit*] The pattern of press corrections in this forme (outer G)
suggests that the proofreader "mis-corrected" here (but cf. II.iii.442.1).
[IV.i]
3. *quite*] completely.

to look us i'th' face, iwis! I wonder with what brow you can
come amongst us. I should seek my fortunes far enough, if
I were you, and neither return to Essex, to be a shame to my   15
predecessors, nor remain about London, to be a mock to my
successors.

QUOMODO [aside].

Subtle Shortyard!

SHORTYARD.

Here are his lands forfeited to us, Master Quomodo; and to
avoid the inconscionable trouble of law, all the assurance   20
he made to us we willingly resign to you.

QUOMODO.

What shall I do with rubbish? Give me money.
'Tis for your worships to have land, that keep great houses;
I should be hoisted.

SHORTYARD.

But, Master Quomodo, if you would but conceive it aright,   25
the land would fall fitter to you than to us.

EASY [aside].

Curts'ing about my land!

SHORTYARD.

You have a towardly son and heir, as we hear.

QUOMODO.

I must needs say, he is a Templar indeed.

SHORTYARD.

We have neither posterity in town, nor hope for any abroad;   30

13. face, iwis!] *Q1* (*cor.*) [! *may be*   18. S.D.] *Dyce.*
bar]; face ywis, *Q1* (*uncor.*), *Q2.*   27. S.D.] *Dyce.*
13. with what] *Q1;* what with *Q2.*

---

13. *iwis*] see II.iii.186, note.
13. *brow*] face, "nerve."
14. *far*] far away.
20. *inconscionable*] see III.iv.174, note.
20. *assurance*] the security (his lands).
24. *hoisted*] in liability for the subsidy (Sampson; see III.iv.175, note).
Cf. Lyly's *Mother Bombie*, II.v.11–12: "he that had a cup of red wine to his
oysters, was hoysted in the Queenes subsidie booke."
27. *Curts'ing*] politely offering to each other (Eccles).
28. *towardly*] promising.
29. *Templar*] see II.iii.410, note.
30. *abroad*] illegitimate children (Price).

we have wives, but the marks have been out of their mouths
these twenty years, and, as it appears, they did little good
when they were in. We could not stand about it, sir; to
get riches and children too, 'tis more than one man can do.
And I am of those citizens' minds that say, let our wives   35
make shift for children and they will, they get none of us;
and I cannot think but he that has both much wealth and
many children, has had more helps coming in than himself.

QUOMODO.

I am not a bow wide of your mind, sir. And for the thrifty
and covetous hopes I have in my son and heir, Sim Quo-   40
modo, that he will never trust his land in wax and parchment, as many gentlemen have done before him—

EASY [aside].

A by-blow for me.

QUOMODO.

I will honestly discharge you, and receive it in due form and
order of law, to strengthen it forever to my son and heir,   45
that he may undoubtedly enter upon't without the let or
molestation of any man, at his or our pleasure whensoever.

SHORTYARD.

'Tis so assur'd unto you.

QUOMODO.

Why, then, Master Easy, y'are a free man, sir; you may deal
in what you please, and go whither you will.   50

[Enter Thomasine.]

39. the] *Q1;* the the *Q2.*   *Q1 (uncor.).*
40–41. Quomodo] *Q2;* Qmomodo   49. free man] *Dyce;* freeman *Q1–2.*
Q1.   50. whither] *Dyce;* whether *Q1–2.*
43. S.D.] *Dyce.*   50.1.] *this edn., relocating Dyce.*
46. upon't] *Q1 (cor.), Q2;* vppon,t

31. *marks*] folds in horses' incisor teeth, which disappeared with age
(Sampson).

36. *make shift*] bestir themselves, contrive.

39. *bow wide*] In archery the distance arrows fell from the target was
measured in bow-lengths (Bullen).

40. *covetous*] see II.iii.160, note.

41–42. *wax and parchment*] sealed legal obligations (Sampson).

43. *by-blow*] side-thrust (Sampson).

46. *let*] hindrance (Dyce).

Why, Thomasine, Master Easy is come from Essex; bid him
welcome in a cup of small beer.

THOMASINE [*aside*].

Not only vild, but in it tyrannous.

QUOMODO.

If it please you, sir, you know the house; you may visit us
often, and dine with us once a quarter.   55

EASY.

Confusion light on you, your wealth, and heir;
Worm gnaw your conscience, as the moth your ware!
I am not the first heir that rob'd or beg'd.

                         Exit [*with* Thomasine].

QUOMODO.

Excellent, excellent, sweet spirits!

SHORTYARD.

Landed Master Quomodo!   60

QUOMODO.

Delicate Shortyard, commodious Falselight,
Hug and away, shift, shift;
'Tis sleight, not strength, that gives the greatest lift.

                    [*Exeunt* Shortyard *and* Falselight.]

Now my desires are full, for this time.
Men may have cormorant wishes, but, alas,   65

53. S.D.] *Dyce.*   63.1.] *Dyce.*
58.1. *with* Thomasine] *this edn.*

---

52. *small*] weak (Sampson).

54. *house*] probably Easy's home in Essex, rather than Quomodo's
shop (where, as Dyce notes, the scene is located).

56–58.] perhaps another aside, but now that all hope is gone it seems
more appropriate for him to attack Quomodo openly, particularly in his
exit speech.

57. *ware*] merchandise, here cloth (cf. II.iii.183).

58.1.] Dyce *seq.* place Thomasine's exit after l. 59; but it seems more
suggestive to have her leave with Easy.

59. S.P.] Kenneth Muir (*Times Literary Supplement*, Feb. 24, 1945, p. 91)
argues that this is Thomasine's praise of Easy; but clearly Quomodo is
addressing Shortyard and Falselight.

61. *commodious*] useful, accommodating.

62–63.] "A trick's the thing" (Price); the imagery (*hug, shift, lift*) is
drawn from wrestling.

65. *cormorant*] insatiably greedy.

A little thing, three hundred pound a year,
Suffices nature, keeps life and soul together!
I'll have 'em lop'd immediately; I long
To warm myself by th' wood.

A fine journey in the Whitsun holidays, i'faith, to ride   70
down with a number of citizens and their wives, some upon
pillions, some upon sidesaddles, I and little Thomasine
i'th' middle, our son and heir, Sim Quomodo, in a peach-
color taffeta jacket, some horse-length or a long yard before
us—there will be a fine show on's, I can tell you—where we   75
citizens will laugh and lie down, get all our wives with
child against a bank, and get up again.

Stay, hah! Hast thou that wit, i'faith? 'Twill be admirable. To see how the very thought of green fields puts a man
into sweet inventions! I will presently possess Sim Quomodo   80
of all the land; I have a toy and I'll do't. And because I
see before mine eyes that most of our heirs prove notorious
rioters after our deaths, and that cozenage in the father
wheels about to folly in the son, our posterity commonly
foil'd at the same weapon at which we play'd rarely; and   85
being the world's beaten word, what's got over the devil's
back (that's by knavery) must be spent under his belly

68–69. I . . . wood] *Dyce; one line in*   72. I] *Q2;* I, *Q1.*
Q1–2.

---

66. *little thing*] ironical.
68. *'em*] his Essex trees (cf. II.iii.339, III.iv.15); *lopping* is cutting off
branches for fuel (Price).
70. *Whitsun*] Whitsunday, the seventh Sunday after Easter.
72. *pillions*] back saddles for a second rider (Schelling).
72. *I*] As Price notes, the Q1 comma suggests "Ay," but all editors
prefer the pronoun (see III.v.54, note).
74. *taffeta*] thin soft silk (Sampson).
74. *long yard*] a cloth measure (Price).
76. *laugh . . . down*] name of a card game (Dyce).
77. *against a bank*] for "a stake of money," according to Sampson; but
see II.iii.85.
80. *possess*] put him in possession.
81. *toy*] see III.i.76, note.
85. *same weapon*] cozenage.
86. *beaten*] well-worn (Bullen; cf. I.ii.11).
86–88. *what's . . . lechery*] proverbial (Tilley, D 316).

(that's by lechery); being awake in these knowings, why
should not I oppose 'em now, and break destiny of her
custom, preventing that by policy, which without it must   90
needs be destiny? And I have took the course; I will forth-
with sicken, call for my keys, make my will, and dispose
of all; give my son this blessing, that he trust no man, keep
his hand from a quean and a scrivener, live in his father's
faith, and do good to nobody. Then will I begin to rave   95
like a fellow of a wide conscience, and, for all the world,
counterfeit to the life that which I know I shall do when I
die: take on for my gold, my lands, and my writings, grow
worse and worse, call upon the devil, and so make an end.

By this time I have indented with a couple of searchers,   100
who, to uphold my device, shall fray them out o'th' chamber
with report of sickness, and so, la, I start up and recover
again. For in this business I will trust, no, not my spirits,
Falselight and Shortyard, but in disguise note the condition
of all: how pitiful my wife takes my death, which will   105
appear by November in her eye, and the fall of the leaf in
her body, but especially by the cost she bestows upon my
funeral, there shall I try her love and regard; my daughter's
marrying to my will and liking; and my son's affection after

---

90. *policy*] crafty calculation.
91. *took the course*] hit on the way to do it (Eccles).
92. *keys*] see II.iii.438, note.
96. *wide conscience*] "wandering reason," according to Sampson, but
more likely "elastic conscience" (Price). Cf. Jonson, Marston, and Chapman's *Eastward Ho*, II.ii.308–309, "a large *Time-fitted* conscience is bound
to nothing," and Jonson's *Every Man Out of His Humor*, Induction, ll.
43–44, where a hypocrite's "conscience/ Is vaster then the ocean."
98. *take on*] grieve (Dyce), carry on.
98. *writings*] legal documents.
100. *By*] before (Price).
100. *indented*] made an agreement (Sampson).
100. *searchers*] appointed to examine corpses and report the cause of
death (Dyce).
101. *fray*] see III.iii.54, note.
102. *sickness*] the plague (Sampson).
106. *November . . . eye*] tears, or bleak "wintery" look.
106. *fall . . . leaf*] autumn; a withering or drooping from grief (Price).
109–110. *affection . . . disposing*] regard for my commands (Sampson).

my disposing; for, to conclude, I am as jealous of this land as   110
of my wife, to know what would become of it after my
decease.   *Exit.*

[IV.ii]   *Enter* Courtesan *with her disguised* Father.

FATHER.

Though I be poor, 'tis my glory to live honest.

COUNTRY WENCH.

I prithee, do not leave me.

FATHER.   To be bawd!
Hell has not such an office.
I thought at first your mind had been preserv'd
In virtue and in modesty of blood,   5
That such a face had not been made to please
The unsettled appetites of several men,
Those eyes turn'd up through prayer, not through lust;
But you are wicked, and my thoughts unjust.

COUNTRY WENCH.

Why, thou art an unreasonable fellow, i'faith. Do not all   10
trades live by their ware, and yet call'd honest livers? Do
they not thrive best when they utter most, and make it
away by the great? Is not wholesale the chiefest merchandise? Do you think some merchants could keep their
wives so brave, but for their wholesale? You're foully   15
deceiv'd and you think so.

FATHER.

You are so glu'd to punishment and shame,
Your words e'en deserve whipping.

IV.ii] *Dyce; no scene division in Q 1–2.*   6–7.] *Dyce; prose in Q 1–2.*
2. S.P.] *Dyce; Curt[ezan]   Q 1–2*   17. punishment] *Q 2;* punishent *Q 1.*
throughout scene.

---

7. *several*] various, different.
9. *unjust*] mistaken (Sampson).
11. *ware*] merchandise.
12. *utter*] sell (Bullen).
12–13. *make . . . great*] dispose of it in large quantities, wholesale
(Sampson).
13,15. *wholesale*] *double-entendre* (Q1–2 read "hole-sale").
15. *brave*] see I.i.297, note.
18. *whipping*] see III.i.174, note.

To bear the habit of a gentlewoman,
And be in mind so distant!   20

COUNTRY WENCH.

Why, you fool you, are not gentlewomen sinners? And
there's no courageous sinner amongst us, but was a gentlewoman by the mother's side, I warrant you. Besides, we are
not always bound to think those our fathers that marry our
mothers, but those that lie with our mothers, and they may   25
be gentlemen born, and born again, for ought we know,
you know.

FATHER.

True, corruption may well be generation's first;
"We're bad by nature, but by custom worst."   *Exeunt.*

[IV.iii]   *A bell tolls; a confused cry within.*

THOMASINE [*within*].

Oh, my husband!

SIM [*within*].

My father, oh, my father!

FALSELIGHT [*within*].

My sweet master, dead!

Enter Shortyard *and the* Boy.

19–20.] *Dyce; prose in Q 1–2.*   IV.iii] *Dyce; no scene division in Q 1–2.*
19. bear] *Q 1* (beare); beart *Q 2.*   1. S.D.] *Dyce.*
28. generation's] *Q 2* (Generations);   2. S.D.] *Dyce.*
Generatious *Q 1.*   3. S.D.] *Dyce.*

---

19. *habit*] clothing, outward appearance.
20. *distant*] far away from gentlehood (Sampson).
22–23. *but . . . side*] She seems to mean that this is every prostitute's
boast (Price).
28. *be . . . first*] presumably, originate in the act of generation (*by nature*).
29. *custom*] habituation. This line has gnomic pointing.
[IV.iii]
0.1.] Dyce *seq.* place this after l. 22, because of l. 4 (Dyce and Bullen
also omit the second clause). But ll. 1–3 are the *cry within*; and, as Price
notes, the *bell* of the S.D. would be the "passing bell" rung for a dying man,
while Shortyard in l. 4 calls for the peal announcing his death. The scene
is located in Quomodo's shop (Dyce).

SHORTYARD.

> Run, boy, bid 'em ring out; he's dead, he's gone.

BOY.

> Then is as arrant a knave gone, as e'er was call'd upon.   5
>   [*Exit.*]

SHORTYARD.

> The happiest good that ever Shortyard felt!
> I want to be express'd, my mirth is such;
> To be struck now, e'en when his joys were high!
> Men only kiss their knaveries, and so die,
> I've often mark'd it.   10
> He was a famous coz'ner while he liv'd,
> And now his son shall reap it; I'll ha' the lands,
> Let him study law after; 'tis no labor
> To undo him forever. But for Easy,
> Only good confidence did make him foolish,   15
> And not the lack of sense, that was not it;
> 'Tis worldly craft beats down a scholar's wit.
> For this our son and heir now, he
> From his conception was entail'd an ass,
> And he has kept it well, twenty-five years now;   20
> Then the slightest art will do't; the lands lie fair;
> "No sin to beggar a deceiver's heir."   *Exit.*

Enter Thomasine *with* Winifred, *her maid, in haste.*

THOMASINE.

> Here, Winifred, here, here, here; I have always found thee
> secret.

5.1.] *Dyce.*

---

5. *arrant*] downright, notorious.
5. *call'd upon*] see III.v.60, note.
7. *want . . . express'd*] lack words to express myself (Sampson).
8. *struck*] see II.iii.77, note.
9.] They die before they can enjoy the fruits of their knaveries.
11.] see Introduction, p. xii, and V.iii.21.
15. *good confidence*] over-trustfulness (cf. I.i.53).
18. *For*] as for.
19. *entail'd*] fixed irrevocably, as an inheritance; cf. Middleton's *Women Beware Women*, II.i.81: "he's a fool entail'd."
20. *it*] the inheritance (his asininity).
22.] gnomic pointing.

WINIFRED.

> You shall always find me so, Mistress.   25

THOMASINE.

> Take this letter and this ring.

WINIFRED.

> Yes, forsooth.

THOMASINE.

> Oh, how all the parts about me shake! Inquire for one
> Master Easy at his old lodging i'th' Blackfriars.

WINIFRED.

> I will indeed, forsooth.   30

THOMASINE.

> Tell him the party that sent him a hundred pound tother
> day to comfort his heart, has likewise sent him this letter
> and this ring, which has that virtue to recover him again
> forever, say. Name nobody, Winifred.

WINIFRED.

> Not so much as you, forsooth.   35

THOMASINE.

> Good girl! Thou shalt have a mourning gown at the burial,
> of mine honesty.

WINIFRED.

> And I'll effect your will, o'my fidelity.   *Exit.*

THOMASINE.

> I do account myself the happiest widow that ever counter-
> feited weeping, in that I have the leisure now both to do   40
> that gentleman good and do myself a pleasure; but I must
> seem like a hanging moon, a little waterish awhile.

Enter Rearage, Courtesan's *Father following.*

29. i'th'] *this edn.;* 'ith the *Q 1–2.*   36. burial,] *this edn.;* buryall *Q 1–2.*
31–32. tother day to] *Q 1;* tother   41. that] *Q 1;* the *Q 2.*
to day *Q 2.*

---

29. *Blackfriars*] district in southwest London (Sampson).

36. *burial,*] Without the comma, *mine honesty* becomes Quomodo, the
one buried (so Price takes it, with misgivings). But this difficulty is removed
if *of* (upon) *mine honesty* is read as a mild oath, echoed in Winifred's *o'my
fidelity* (1. 38).

42. *hanging moon*] the rainy crescent moon that "will not hold water"
(Price).

REARAGE.

I entertain both thee and thy device;

'Twill put 'em both to shame.

FATHER.   That is my hope, sir,

Especially that strumpet.   [*Exit.*]

REARAGE.   Save you, sweet widow!   45

I suffer for your heaviness.

THOMASINE.

Oh, Master Rearage, I have lost the dearest husband that
ever woman did enjoy.

REARAGE.

You must have patience yet.

THOMASINE.

Oh, talk not to me of patience and you love me, good Master   50
Rearage.

REARAGE.

Yet, if all tongues go right, he did not use you so well as a
man mought.

THOMASINE.

Nay, that's true indeed, Master Rearage; he ne'er us'd me so
well as a woman might have been us'd, that's certain; in   55
troth, 't'as been our greatest falling out, sir; and though
it be the part of a widow to show herself a woman for her
husband's death, yet when I remember all his unkindness, I
cannot weep a stroke, i'faith, Master Rearage. And therefore wisely did a great widow in this land comfort up   60
another: "Go to, lady," quoth she, "leave blubbering; thou
thinkest upon thy husband's good parts when thou sheddest
tears; do but remember how often he has lain from thee, and
how many naughty slippery turns he has done thee, and
thou wilt ne'er weep for him, I warrant thee." You would   65
not think how that counsel has wrought with me, Master

45. S.D.] *Price.*

---

43. *entertain*] receive, accept.

44. *'em*] Lethe and the Country Wench.

45. S.D.] Perhaps by oversight, Dyce *seq.* provide no exit for the Father
until the end of the scene.

53. *mought*] might.

57. *show . . . woman*] weep (Schelling).

66. *wrought with*] worked upon, affected.

Rearage; I could not dispend another tear now, and you
would give me ne'er so much.

REARAGE.

Why, I count you the wiser widow; it shows you have
wisdom, when you can check your passion. For mine own 70
part, I have no sense to sorrow for his death, whose life was
the only rub to my affection.

THOMASINE.

Troth, and so it was to mine; but take courage now; you're
a landed gentleman, and my daughter is seven hundred
pound strong to join with you. 75

REARAGE.

But Lethe lies i'th' way.

THOMASINE.   Let him lie still;
You shall tread o'er him or I'll fail in will.

REARAGE.

Sweet widow!   *Exeunt.*

[IV.iv]   *Enter* Quomodo *like a Beadle.*

QUOMODO.

What a belov'd man did I live! My servants gall their
fingers with wringing, my wife's cheeks smart with weeping,
tears stand in every corner; you may take water in my
house. But am not I a wise fool now? What if my wife
should take my death so to heart that she should sicken 5

---

76. Lethe lies i'th'] *Q 1;* Lethes 'th
Q 2.
IV.iv] *Dyce; no scene division in
Q 1-2.*

2. wringing] *this edn.;* ringing *Q 1-2.*
3. tears] *catch-word in Q 1-2, not in
text.*

---

67. *dispend*] expend.
71. *sense*] feeling (Price).
72. *rub*] obstacle, a term borrowed from bowling (Bullen).
74-75. *seven hundred pound*] her dowry (cf. III.i.204, V.iii.112-113).
77. *in will*] in getting my way.
[IV.iv]
0.1. *Beadle*] see III.v.16, note.
1. *gall*] make sore by chafing.
2. *wringing*] Dyce (and apparently the other editors) assume they were
ringing the church bells, which is most unlikely.
3. *take water*] travel by boat (Eccles).

upon't, nay, swoon, nay, die? When did I hear of a woman
do so? Let me see. Now I remember me, I think 'twas before
my time; yes, I have heard of those wives that have wept,
and sob'd, and swoon'd; marry, I never heard but they recovered again; that's a comfort, la, that's a comfort, and I   10
hope so will mine. Peace, 'tis near upon the time, I see; here
comes the worshipful Livery; I have the Hospital Boys; I
perceive little Thomasine will bestow cost of me.—
I'll listen to the common censure now,
How the world tongues me when my ear lies low.   15

Enter the Livery [*and the Hospital Boys*].

FIRST LIVERYMAN.
   Who, Quomodo? Merely enrich'd by shifts
   And coz'nages, believe it.
QUOMODO [*aside*].
   I see the world is very loath to praise me,
   'Tis rawly friends with me; I cannot blame it,
   For what I have done has been to vex and shame it.   20
   Here comes my son, the hope, the landed heir,
   One whose rare thrift will say, "Men's tongues, you lie;
   I'll keep by law what was got craftily."

[*Enter* Sim.]

   Methinks I hear him say so.
   He does salute the Livery with good grace   25
   And solemn gesture.—

14–15.] *Dyce; prose in Q 1–2.*   18. S.D.] *Dyce.*
15.1 *and the Hospital Boys*] *Price*   22. One] *Q 2*; Ont *Q 1.*
(*subs.*).   23.1.] *Dyce.*

---

   11. *time*] for the funeral. The scene, Dyce notes, is located outside
Quomodo's shop. The procession—first the *Livery* (cf. II.iii.415) and
Hospital Boys (from Christ's Hospital, hired to sing at funerals), and then
the coffin, followed by the Mourners—forms at his door and passes over the
stage on its way to church (l. 38), as Price explains.
   14. *censure*] judgment (Bullen).
   15. *tongues me*] speaks of me.
   16. *Who*] presumably replying to a question by another member of the
guild (Price).
   19. *rawly*] barely, imperfectly (Price).
   22. *Men's tongues*] "the world's beaten word" of IV.i.86–88.

[*To him.*] Oh, my young worshipful master, you have
parted from a dear father, a wise and provident father.

SIM.

Art thou grown an ass now?

QUOMODO.

Such an honest father—   30

SIM.

Prithee, beadle, leave thy lying; I am scarce able to endure
thee, i'faith; what honesty didst thou e'er know by my
father? Speak! Rule your tongue, beadle, lest I make you
prove it, and then I know what will become of you; 'tis the
scurviest thing i'th' earth to belie the dead so, and he's a   35
beastly son and heir that will stand by and hear his father
belied to his face; he will ne'er prosper, I warrant him.
Troth, if I be not asham'd to go to church with him, I would
I might be hang'd; I hear such filthy tales go on him. Oh,
if I had known he had been such a lewd fellow in his life,   40
he should ne'er have kept me company.

QUOMODO [*aside*].

Oh, oh, oh!

SIM.

But I am glad he's gone, though 'twere long first; Shortyard
and I will revel it, i'faith; I have made him my rent-
gatherer already.   45

QUOMODO [*aside*].

He shall be speedily disinherited;
He gets not a foot, not the crown of a molehill.
I'll sooner make a courtier my heir,
For teaching my wife tricks, than thee,

27. S.D.] *this edn.;* S.P. *Bead*[*le*]   42. S.D.] *Dyce.*
Q 1–2.   46. S.D.] *Dyce.*
30. S.P.] *Dyce; Bead*[*le*] *Q 1–2.*   46–47.] *this edn.; prose in Q 1–2.*
33. lest] *Q 2;* least *Q 1.*   48–53.] *Price; prose in Q 1–2.*
39. hear] *Q 2;* feare *Q 1.*

27–28.] These lines (and l. 30; see textual note) could be spoken by
another Beadle in the procession, but all editors assume Quomodo is meant
(see V.i.78, note).
40. *lewd*] vile, base (Dyce).
43. *'twere long first*] it took a long time (Sampson).
47. *foot*] of his land.   47. *crown*] top.

My most neglectful son!   50
Oh, now the corse, I shall observe yet farther.

A counterfeit corse brought in, [followed by] Thomasine *and all the Mourners
equally counterfeit.*

Oh, my most modest, virtuous, and rememb'ring wife,
She shall have all when I die, she shall have all.

Enter Easy.

THOMASINE [*aside*].
Master Easy? 'Tis. Oh, what shift shall I make now?
—Oh!   *Falls down in a feigned swoon.*   55
QUOMODO [*aside*].
Sweet wife, she swoons; I'll let her alone; I'll have no mercy
at this time; I'll not see her, I'll follow the corse.   *Exit.*
EASY [*to corse*].
The devil grind thy bones, thou coz'ning rascal!
MOTHER.
Give her a little more air; tilt up her head. —Comfort
thyself, good widow; do not fall like a beast for a husband;   60
there's more than we can well tell where to put 'em, good
soul.
THOMASINE.
Oh, I shall be well anon.
MOTHER.
Fie, you have no patience, i'faith. I have buried four
husbands, and never offered 'em such abuse.   65
THOMASINE [*to* Easy].
Cousin, how do you?
EASY.   Sorry to see you ill, coz.
THOMASINE.
The worst is past, I hope.   *Pointing after the coffin.*
EASY.   I hope so too.

54. S.D.] *Dyce.*	58. S.D.] *Price (subs.).*
56. S.D.] *Dyce.*	66. S.D.] *this edn.*

51. *corse*] corpse.
59. S.P.] Dyce *seq.* make her Thomasine's mother; but Price points
out that her lines (especially ll. 64–65) do not suggest this, and that she is
probably just an older neighbor.
66. *Cousin*] merely a familiar mode of address (Bullen).

THOMASINE.

 Lend me your hand, sweet coz, I have troubled you.

MOTHER.

 No trouble indeed, forsooth. —[*To* Easy.] Good cousin,
 have a care of her; comfort her up as much as you can, and 70
 all little enough, I warrant ye. *Exeunt* [Mother *and Mourners*].

THOMASINE.

 My most sweet love!

EASY.   My life is not so dear.

THOMASINE.

 I have always pitied you.

EASY.   Y'ave shown it here,
 And given the desperate hope!

THOMASINE.   Delay not now,
 Y'ave understood my love; I have a priest ready;   75
 This is the fittest season, no eye offends us,
 Let this kiss
 Restore thee to more wealth, me to more bliss.

EASY.

 The angels have provided for me.   [*Exeunt.*]

    Finit Actus Quartus.

[V.i]

  Enter Shortyard *with writings, having cozen'd Sim Quomodo.*

SHORTYARD.

 I have not scope enough within my breast

---

69. S.D.] *this edn.*   *Dyce; prose in* Q 1–2.
71. S.D. Mother *and Mourners*] 79.1. *Finit*] *this edn.; Finis* Q 1–2.
Price.   V.i] *Incipit Quintus et Ultimus* Q 1–2.
74–76. Delay . . . us] *Price, revising*

---

 68. *your hand*] to help her up; but Sampson notes that the taking of
hands was a legal formality to a betrothal.
 69. *No trouble*] She seems to think Thomasine was apologizing to her
(Price).
 71. S.D.] Dyce *seq.* have the coffin and Mourners leave at l. 55 (and so
change the quarto *Exeunt* here to "Exit"). But the coffin is still on stage at
l. 58, apparently just passing from view at l. 67, and the Mourners follow it.
 76. *offends*] by watching.
[V.i]
 0.1. *writings*] Quomodo's legal papers, which Sim inherited.

To keep my joys contain'd; I'm Quomodo's heir,
The lands, assurances, and all are mine;
I have trip'd his son's heels up above the ground
His father left him. Had I not encouragement?   5
Do not I know, what proves the father's prey,
The son ne'er looks on't, but it melts away?
Do not I know, the wealth that's got by fraud,
Slaves share it like the riches of a bawd?
Why, 'tis a curse unquenchable, ne'er cools.   10
Knaves still commit their consciences to fools,
And they betray who ow'd 'em. Here's all the bonds,
All Easy's writings; let me see.

Enter Quomodo's wife, [Thomasine,] *married to* Easy.

THOMASINE.

Now my desires wear crowns.

EASY.   My joys exceed;
Man is ne'er healthful till his follies bleed.   15

THOMASINE.

Oh, behold the villain, who in all those shapes
Confounded your estate!

EASY.   That slave! That villain!

SHORTYARD [*reading*].

"So many acres of good meadow—"

EASY.   Rascal!

SHORTYARD.

I hear you, sir.

EASY.

Rogue, Shortyard, Blastfield, sergeant, deputy, coz'ner!   20

2. heir] *Dyce; begins l. 3 in* Q*1–2.*

---

3. *assurances*] deeds, titles (Sampson); cf. IV.i.20.
7. *son*] punning on "sun."
11. *consciences*] minds, hearts (Price); or it may be figurative: they pawn their consciences (cf. IV.i.96) to enrich the *fools* (their heirs), counting on them to justify this immoral course by their thrift, etc. (cf. IV.iv.21–23).
12. *ow'd*] owned; i.e., the fools betray the knaves (Price).
14. *exceed*] are surpassing (Eccles).
15.] Many illnesses were treated by bleeding the patient.
16. *shapes*] disguises (Sampson).
20. *deputy*] his last disguise (III.iv.178).

SHORTYARD.

Hold, hold!

EASY.

I thirst the execution of his ears.

THOMASINE.

Hate you that office.

EASY.

I'll strip him bare for punishment and shame.

SHORTYARD.

Why, do but hear me, sir; you will not think   25
What I have done for you.

EASY.   Given his son my lands!

SHORTYARD.

Why, look you, 'tis not so, you're not told true;
I have cozen'd him again merely for you,
Merely for you, sir; 'twas my meaning then
That you should wed her, and have all again.   30
O'my troth, it's true, sir; look you then here, sir.

[*Giving the writings.*]

You shall not miss a little scroll, sir. Pray, sir,
Let not the city know me for a knave;
There be richer men would envy my preferment,
If I should be known before 'em.   35

EASY.

Villain, my hate to more revenge is drawn;
When slaves are found, 'tis their base art to fawn.—
Within there!

[*Enter Officers.*]

SHORTYARD.

How now? Fresh warders!

25–26. Why . . . you] *Dyce;* prose in   31.1.] *Dyce.*
Q 1–2.   38.1.] *this edn.*
31–35.] *Dyce;* prose in Q 1–2.

22. *ears*] Some punishments included the cutting off of the culprit's
ears by the public executioner (*that office*, l. 23).
32. *little scroll*] single paper (Schelling).
34. *preferment*] see I.ii.16, note (ironical here).
35. *known before*] ranked ahead of (in knavery).
37. *found*] found out (cf. l. 40).
39. *Fresh warders*] more guards (Schelling).

EASY.

This is the other, bind him fast. —Have I found you,   40
Master Blastfield?

SHORTYARD.   This is the fruit of craft.

Like him that shoots up high, looks for the shaft,
And finds it in his forehead, so does hit
The arrow of our fate; wit destroys wit;
The head the body's bane and his own bears.—   45
You ha' corn enough, you need not reap mine ears.

EASY.

Sweet Master Blastfield! —I loathe his voice; away!

                                    Exit [Shortyard *with Officers*].

THOMASINE.

What happiness was here! But are you sure
You have all?

EASY.   I hope so, my sweet wife.

THOMASINE.

What difference there is in husbands, not only in one thing, 50
but in all.

EASY.

Here's good deeds and bad deeds, the writings that keep my
lands to me, and the bonds that gave it away from me.
These, my good deeds, shall to more safety turn,
And these, my bad, have their deserts and burn.   55
I'll see thee again presently; read there.   [*Exit.*]

---

47. Sweet Master Blastfield] *Price*   48–49. What . . . all?] *this edn.; prose*
conj.; ends Shortyard's speech in Q 1–2.   *in Q 1–2.*
                                        56. S.D.] *Dyce.*

---

40. *other*] He already had them arrest Falselight. Dyce *seq.* have the
Officers bring him in at l. 38.1, and carry them both off at l. 47.1, since
they appear together in V.iii; but it is not likely that Shortyard would
completely ignore his partner here.

42. *shaft*] arrow.

45.] The *head*, by losing its ears, bears punishment for body and brain
(Price); or this may expand l. 44: the cozener's wit (*head*) causes the
destruction (*bears* the *bane*) of itself and his body.

46. *corn*] grain, i.e., wealth.

47. *Sweet Master Blastfield*] Sampson corrects the quarto by substituting
"Easy" for *Blastfield*; but the emendation here (suggested by Price, though
he prefers Sampson's) is less drastic, and consistent with Easy's sarcasm in
l. 41.

52. *deeds*] legal papers (cf. II.iii.351), and actions.

THOMASINE.

Did he want all, who would not love his care?

Enter Quomodo [*like a Beadle*].

QUOMODO [*aside*].

What a wife hast thou, Ephestian Quomodo! So loving, so
mindful of her duty, not only seen to weep, but known to
swoon! I knew a widow about Saint Antlings so forgetful of   60
her first husband that she married again within the twelve-
month; nay, some, by'rlady, within the month; there were
sights to be seen! Had they my wife's true sorrows, seven
months nor seven years would draw 'em to the stake. I would
most tradesmen had such a wife as I; they hope they have,   65
we must all hope the best. Thus in her honor:

> A modest wife is such a jewel,
> Every goldsmith cannot show it;
> He that's honest and not cruel
> Is the likeliest man to owe it.   70

And that's I; I made it by myself; and coming to her as a
beadle for my reward this morning, I'll see how she takes
my death next her heart.

THOMASINE.

Now, beadle.

QUOMODO.

Bless your mistress-ship's eyes from too many tears,   75
Although you have lost a wise and worshipful gentleman.

THOMASINE.

You come for your due, beadle, here i'th' house?

58. S.D.] *Dyce.*   64. months] *Dyce; not in Q 1–2.*

---

56. *there*] giving her the papers, which she reads during Quomodo's
soliloquy (Dyce's S.D.).

57. *Did . . . all*] even if he had nothing.

60. *Saint Antlings*] St. Antholin's Church in Budge Row, known as a
Puritan stronghold (Sugden).

63–64. *seven months*] "not" or "neither" understood.

68. *Every . . . cannot*] not every one can (Schelling).

70. *owe*] own, admit ("own up").

72. *reward*] payment, his *due* (l. 77).

77. *house*] The scene is located in Quomodo's shop (Dyce).

QUOMODO.

> Most certain; the Hospital money, and mine own poor forty
> pence.

THOMASINE.

> I must crave a discharge from you, beadle.   80

QUOMODO.

> Call your man; I'll heartily set my hand to a memorandum.

THOMASINE.

> You deal the trulier.

QUOMODO [*aside*].

> Good wench still.

THOMASINE.

> George!

> *[Enter Servant.]*

> Here is the beadle come for his money; draw a memoran-   85
> dum that he has received all his due he can claim here i'th'
> house after this funeral.

QUOMODO [*aside, while Servant writes*].

> What politic directions she gives him, all to secure herself!
> 'Tis time, i'faith, now to pity her; I'll discover myself to her
> ere I go; but came it off with some lively jest now, that were   90
> admirable. I have it! After the memorandum is written and
> all, I'll set my own name to't, Ephestian Quomodo; she'll
> start, she'll wonder how Ephestian Quomodo came thither,
> that was buried yesterday. Y'are beset, little Quomodo.

83. S.D.] *Dyce.*	93. thither] *Q 1* (thether); hither
84.1.] *Dyce.*	*Q 2, Dyce seq.*
88. S.D.] *Dyce.*	94. Quomodo] *Q 2*; Qnomodo *Q 1.*
92. I'll] *Q 2;* lle *Q 1.*	

---

78. *Hospital money*] singers' fee (see IV.iv.11, note).

78. *mine own*] his fee for officiating at the funeral—further evidence that
he is the Beadle of IV.iv.27.

80. *discharge*] receipt (Sampson), release.

88. *politic*] see III.v.16, note.

89. *discover*] reveal.

93. *thither*] there, on the memorandum (Price).

94. *beset*] see III.iii.9, note.

94. *little Quomodo*] Thomasine; see Dramatis Personae, l. 14, note, and
II.iii.396, IV.i.72, IV.iv.13.

THOMASINE [*counting out money*].

    Nineteen, twenty; five pound; one, two, three; and four-   95
    pence.

QUOMODO [*aside, while signing*].

    So, we shall have good sport when 'tis read.   [*Exit Servant.*]

[*Enter* Easy.]

EASY.

    How now, lady, paying away money so fast?

THOMASINE.

    The beadle's due here, sir.

QUOMODO [*aside*].

    Who? 'Tis Easy! What makes Easy in my house?   100
    He is not my wife's overseer, I hope.

EASY.

    What's here?

QUOMODO [*aside*].

    He makes me sweat.

EASY [*reading*].

    "Memorandum: that I have received of Richard Easy all
    my due I can claim here i'th' house, or any hereafter for   105
    me. In witness whereof I have set to mine own hand:
    Ephestian Quomodo."

QUOMODO [*aside*].

    What have I done? Was I mad?

95. S.D.] *this edn.*
97. S.D.] *both by Dyce (subs.)*.
97.1.] *Dyce (subs.)*.
100. S.D.] *Dyce.*

100. Who? 'Tis] *Price conj.;* Whose?
tis *Q1;* Who's? this *Q2;* Who's
this?/ 'Tis *Dyce seq.*
103. S.D.] *Dyce.*
108. S.D.] *Dyce.*

---

    95. S.D.] "Running over the memorandum" in Dyce *seq.*; but the paper
specifies no sums—that is the whole point (see V.iii.63). She counts out
the coins to be paid over: *nineteen, twenty* (and *one, two, three*) are shillings
(20*s.* = £1). Since the beadle got 3 shillings 4 pence (40 pence; 12 pence =
1*s.*), £5 is the Hospital fee.
    100. *Who? 'Tis*] see I.i.142, note. Price's argument is less convincing
here, because of the ? in Q1, but it still seems the best alternative.
    101. *overseer*] steward (Sampson).
    105. *any*] anyone.

EASY.

    Ephestian Quomodo?

QUOMODO.

    Ay, well, what then, sir? Get you out of my house   110
    First, you Master Prodigal Had-land; away!

THOMASINE.

    What, is the beadle drunk or mad?
    Where are my men to thrust him out o'doors?

QUOMODO.

    Not so, good Thomasine, not so.

THOMASINE.

    This fellow must be whip'd.

QUOMODO.   Thank you, good wife.   115

EASY.

    I can no longer bear him.

THOMASINE.   Nay, sweet husband.

QUOMODO [aside].

    Husband? I'm undone, beggar'd, cozen'd, confounded
    forever! Married already? —Will it please you know me
    now, Mistress Harlot and Master Horner? Who am I now?

                                     [Discovers himself.]

THOMASINE.

    Oh, he's as like my tother husband as can be.   120

QUOMODO.

    I'll have judgment; I'll bring you before a judge; you shall
    feel, wife, whether my flesh be dead or no; I'll tickle you,
    i'faith, i'faith.   Exit.

THOMASINE.

    The judge that he'll solicit knows me well.

EASY.

    Let's on then, and our grievances first tell.   Exeunt. 125

110–111. house/ First,] Price;   117. S.D.] Dyce.
house,/ First Q1–2; house first,/   119.1.] Dyce.
Dyce seq.

---

    111. First] apparently, before I proceed any further; but it may belong
to the next clause (see textual note).
    111. Had-land] slang name for a prodigal (Sampson); Dyce cites Middle-
ton's A Trick to Catch the Old One, I.ii.4: "bully Had-land."
    119. Horner] since he has given Quomodo horns, i.e., made him a cuckold.

[V.ii]

Enter Lethe *with Officers, taken with his* Harlot; [Rearage *and* Susan *looking on*].

REARAGE.

Here they come.

SUSAN.   Oh, where?

LETHE.   Heart of shame!

Upon my wedding morning, so disgrac'd!

Have you so little conscience, officers,

You will not take a bribe?

COUNTRY WENCH.

Master Lethe, we may lie together lawfully hereafter, for   5
we are coupled together before people enow, i'faith.

[*Exeunt Officers with* Lethe *and his* Harlot.]

REARAGE.

There goes the strumpet.

SUSAN.

Pardon my willful blindness, and enjoy me;

For now the difference appears too plain

Betwixt a base slave and a true gentleman.   10

REARAGE.

I do embrace thee in the best of love.—

[*Aside.*] How soon affections fail, how soon they prove!

[*Exeunt.*]

V.ii] *Dyce; no scene division in Q 1–2.*   5. S.P.] *Dyce; Cur[tezan] Q 1–2.*
0.1–2. Rearage . . . on] *this edn.*   6.1.] *Dyce (subs.).*
1–2. Heart . . . disgrac'd] *Dyce; one*   12. S.D.] *this edn.*
line in Q 1–2.

0.1.] Dyce *seq.* add Salewood, Hellgill, and Mother Gruel to this S.D. (which they place after Susan's speech), since they enter with Lethe and the Wench in V.iii (cf. V.i.40, note). As Price explains, this scene is the result of Rearage's plot in IV.iii.43; he has had Lethe and the Wench arrested, on the morning that Lethe was to marry Susan, and now brings Susan to see them being led off through the streets to the Judge.

4. *bribe*] to let him go.

8. *enjoy me*] as your wife.

12.] How soon such feelings as love vanish, how soon they spring up for another (Eccles); but, as Price notes, this is not very complimentary to Susan, hence it is made an aside here.

[V.iii]

Enter Judge, Easy *and* Thomasine *in talk with him;* [Shortyard *and*
Falselight *in the custody of Officers*].

JUDGE.

His coz'nages are odious; he the plaintiff!
Not only fram'd deceitful in his life,
But so to mock his funeral!

EASY.   Most just.

The Livery all assembled, mourning weeds
Throughout his house e'en down to his last servant,   5
The herald richly hir'd to lend him arms
Feign'd from his ancestors, which I dare swear knew
No other arms but those they labor'd with,
All preparations furnish'd, nothing wanted
Save that which was the cause of all: his death.   10
If he be living!

JUDGE.   'Twas an impious part.

EASY.

We are not certain yet it is himself,
But some false spirit that assumes his shape
And seeks still to deceive me.

[*Enter* Quomodo.]

QUOMODO.   Oh, are you come?—
My lord! —They're here. Good morrow, Thomasine.   15

V.iii] *Dyce; no scene division in Q 1–2.*   14–15. Oh . . . Thomasine] *Dyce;*
0.1–2. Shortyard . . . *Officers*] *Dyce.*   *prose in Q 1–2.*
8. No] *Dyce; ends l. 7 in Q 1–2.*   15. lord!] *Q 1* (Lord?); Lord, *Q 2,*
14. S.D.] *Dyce.*   *Dyce seq.*
                                                    15. They're] *Q 2;* their *Q 1.*

0.1.] The scene is located in the Judge's house (Dyce).
3. *just*] correct (see IV.ii.9, note).
4. *weeds*] clothes (cf. Induction, l. 2).
6. *richly*] at great expense (Schelling); i.e., bribed.
6. *arms*] a coat of arms, the badge of gentility, the use of which was
regulated by the *herald* (with a pun on "limbs," l. 8).
7. *from*] as inherited from.   11. *part*] proceeding (Schelling).
13. *spirit*] see Introduction, p. xvii.
14. *you*] probably Easy and Thomasine; then *They* (l. 15) would be
Shortyard and Falselight (Price).
15. *lord!*] As Price notes, the Q2 comma (adopted in Dyce *seq.*) has him
announce to the Judge what he must already know.

JUDGE.

> Now, what are you?

QUOMODO.

> I am Quomodo, my lord, and this my wife;
> Those my two men, that are bound wrongfully.

JUDGE.

> How are we sure y'are he?

QUOMODO.

> Oh, you cannot miss, my lord.

JUDGE.   I'll try you;   20

> Are you the man that liv'd the famous coz'ner?

QUOMODO.

> Oh, no, my lord.

JUDGE.

> Did you deceive this gentleman of his right,
> And laid nets o'er his land?

QUOMODO.   Not I, my lord.

JUDGE.

> Then y'are not Quomodo, but a counterfeit.—   25
> [*To Officers.*] Lay hands on him, and bear him to the whip.

QUOMODO.

> Stay, stay a little,
> I pray; now I remember me, my lord,
> I cozen'd him indeed, 'tis wondrous true.

JUDGE.

> Then I dare swear this is no counterfeit.   30
> Let all doubts cease; this man is Quomodo.

QUOMODO.

> Why, la, you now, you would not believe this?
> I am found what I am.

JUDGE.

> But setting these thy odious shifts apart,
> Why did that thought profane enter thy breast   35
> To mock the world with thy supposed death?

QUOMODO.

> Conceive you not that, my lord? A policy.

26. S.D.] *this edn.*
27–28.] *Dyce; one line in Q 1–2.*
28. I pray] *Q1;* pray *Q2.*

30. counterfeit] *Q 1 (cor.), Q 2;*
connterfet *Q 1 (uncor.).*
32–33.] *Dyce; prose in Q 1–2.*

33.] I am found to be myself.   37. *policy*] see IV.i.90, note.

JUDGE.

    So.

QUOMODO.

    For, having gotten the lands, I thirsted still

    To know what fate would follow 'em.   40

JUDGE.

    Being ill got.

QUOMODO.   Your lordship apprehends me.

JUDGE.

    I think I shall anon.

QUOMODO.   And thereupon

    I, out of policy, possess'd my son,

    Which since I have found lewd, and now intend

    To disinherit him forever.   45

    Not only this was in my death set down,

    But thereby a firm trial of my wife,

    Her constant sorrows, her rememb'ring virtues;

    All which are dews; the shine of a next morning

    Dries 'em up all, I see't.   50

JUDGE.

    Did you profess wise cozenage, and would dare

    To put a woman to her two days' choice,

    When oft a minute does it?

QUOMODO.   Less, a moment,

    The twinkling of an eye, a glimpse, scarce something does it.

    Your lordship yet will grant she is my wife?   55

THOMASINE.

    Oh, heaven!

JUDGE.

    After some penance, and the dues of law,

    I must acknowledge that.

QUOMODO.   I scarce like

    Those dues of law.

49–50.] *Dyce; prose in Q1–2.*   50. see't] *Q1;* see it *Q2.*

---

    41. *apprehends*] understands; but the Judge takes it in the sense of "arrests."

    44. *lewd*] see IV.iv.40, note.

    46. *set down*] as part of his plan.

    49. *shine*] sunshine, which dries up the *dews* (her tears).

    51. *profess*] claim to practice.

EASY.   My lord,

    Although the law too gently 'lot his wife,   60
    The wealth he left behind he cannot challenge.

QUOMODO.

    How?

EASY.

    Behold his hand against it.   *[Showing memorandum.]*

QUOMODO [*aside*].

    He does devise all means to make me mad,
    That I may no more lie with my wife   65
    In perfect memory; I know't, but yet
    The lands will maintain me in my wits;
    The land will do so much for me.

JUDGE [*reading*].

    "In witness whereof I have set to mine own hand: *Ephestian*
    Quomodo."   70
    'Tis firm enough your own, sir.

QUOMODO.

    A jest, my lord; I did I knew not what.

JUDGE.

    It should seem so; deceit is her own foe,
    Craftily gets, and childishly lets go.
    But yet the lands are his.

QUOMODO.   I warrant ye.   75

EASY.

    No, my good lord, the lands know the right heir;
    I am their master once more.

QUOMODO.   Have you the lands?

59–60. My . . . wife] *Dyce; one line*   64–68.] *Dyce; prose in Q 1–2.*
in Q 1–2.   72. knew] *Q 1;* know *Q 2.*
63. S.D.] *Price.*   75. I] *Q 2;* I, *Q 1.*
64. S.D.] *this edn.*   77. lands] *Q 1;* land *Q 2.*

---

  60. *'lot*] allot, assign.
  61. *challenge*] claim (challenge my right to it).
  66. *memory*] knowing she has slept with another (cf. V.i.119).
  68. *land*] Dyce *seq.* emend to *lands,* perhaps correctly.
  75. *lands are his*] the lands in Essex are Quomodo's (since the memorandum only covered the shop).
  75. *I*] The Q1 comma suggests "Ay" (see III.v.54, note); but the phrase *I warrant* has been used throughout the play.

EASY.

　　Yes, truly, I praise heaven.

QUOMODO.　　　　　　　　　Is this good dealing?

　　Are there such consciences abroad? How,

　　Which way could he come by 'em?

SHORTYARD.　　　　　　　　　My lord,　　　　　　80

　　I'll quickly resolve you that, it comes to me.

　　This coz'ner, whom too long I call'd my patron,

　　To my thought dying, and the fool, his son,

　　Possess'd of all, which my brain partly sweat for,

　　I held it my best virtue, by a plot　　　　　　85

　　To get from him what for him was ill got—

QUOMODO.

　　Oh, beastly Shortyard!

SHORTYARD.　　　　　　　When, no sooner mine,

　　But I was glad more quickly to resign.

JUDGE.

　　Craft, once discover'd, shows her abject line.

QUOMODO [aside].

　　He hits me everywhere, for craft, once known,　　90

　　Does teach fools wit, leaves the deceiver none.

　　My deeds have cleft me, cleft me!

Enter Officers *with* Lethe *and the* Harlot, [*followed by* Rearage, Salewood, Hellgill, Mother Gruel, *and Susan*].

FIRST OFFICER.

　　Room there!

QUOMODO [aside].　　A little yet to raise my spirit;

78–80. Is . . . 'em] *Dyce; prose in
Q1–2.*
80–81. My . . . me] *Dyce; one line in
Q1–2.*
81. you that,] *this edn.;* you, that
Q1–2; you that *Dyce seq.*

86. for] *Q1;* from *Q2.*
90. S.D.] *Dyce.*
92.1–2. *followed . . . Susan*]　　*Dyce
(subs.).*
93. S.D.] *this edn.*

　　81. *resolve*] explain (Schelling).
　　81. *that,*] Without the comma, Shortyard's promise is too restricted.
He will explain *that,* i.e., how Easy got the land; *it* could refer to the
means, or to the question itself.
　　83. *To my thought*] as I thought (Sampson).
　　89. *abject line*] vile course (Price).

Here Master Lethe comes to wed my daughter;
That's all the joy is left me. —Hah! Who's this?   95

JUDGE.

What crimes have those brought forth?

SALEWOOD.   The shame of lust;
Most viciously on this, his wedding morning,
This man was seiz'd in shame with that bold strumpet.

JUDGE.

Why, 'tis she he means to marry.

LETHE.   No, in truth.

JUDGE.

In truth, you do;   100
Who, for his wife, his harlot doth prefer,
Good reason 'tis that he should marry her.

COUNTRY WENCH.

I crave it on my knees; such was his vow at first.

HELLGILL [*aside*].

I'll say so too, and work out mine own safety.—
Such was his vow at first, indeed, my lord,   105
Howe'er his mood has chang'd him!

LETHE.   Oh, vild slave!

COUNTRY WENCH.

He says it true, my lord.

JUDGE.   Rest content,
He shall both marry and taste punishment.

LETHE.

Oh, intolerable! I beseech your good lordship, if I must
have an outward punishment, let me not marry an inward, 110
whose lashes will ne'er out, but grow worse and worse. I
have a wife stays for me this morning with seven hundred

---

96. S.P. SALEWOOD] *Dyce; Gent[le-
man] Q 1–2.*
103. S.P.] *Dyce; Curt[ezan] Q 1–2.*
104. S.P.] *Dyce; Pand[er] Q 1–2.*
104. S.D.] *Dyce.*
104. I'll . . . too] *Dyce; separate line*

in Q 1–2.
107. S.P.] *Dyce; Curt[ezan] Q 1–2.*
109. Oh, intolerable] *Dyce; separate
line in Q 1–2.*
111. lashes] *Q 2; lastes Q 1.*

---

96. S.P. *Salewood*] All editors agree this is Salewood (also at l. 115), who
is Rearage's partner in this plot (see III.v.1–5, 57).
101. *for*] instead of (Price).
103. *at first*] when he seduced her.
111. *lashes . . . out*] whip-marks will never disappear.

pound in her purse; let me be speedily whip'd and be gone,
I beseech your lordship.

SALEWOOD.

    He speaks no truth, my lord; behold the virgin,   115
    Wife to a well-esteemed gentleman,
    Loathing the sin he follows.

LETHE.

    I was betrayed, yes, faith.

REARAGE.

    . . . His own mother, my lord,
    Which he confess'd, through ignorance and disdain,   120
    His name so chang'd to abuse the world and her.

LETHE [aside].

    Marry a harlot, why not? 'Tis an honest man's fortune. I
    pray, did not one of my countrymen marry my sister? Why,
    well then, if none should be married but those that are
    honest, where should a man seek a wife after Christmas? I   125
    pity that gentleman that has nine daughters to bestow,
    and seven of 'em seeded already; they will be good stuff by
    that time.—

    I do beseech your lordship to remove
    The punishment; I am content to marry her.   130

JUDGE.

    There's no removing of your punishment—

LETHE.

    Oh, good my lord!

JUDGE.   Unless one here assembled,

115. S.P.] *Dyce; Gent[leman]* Q*1–2.*   129–130.] *Dyce; prose in* Q*1–2.*
122. S.D.] *this edn.*

---

    115. *virgin*] Susan, who has remained in the background, married
Rearage just before this scene (see V.ii.8).
    117. *sin he follows*] Lethe's lust.
    119–121.] This is corrupt. As Price notes, Rearage is explaining to the
Judge, in an aside, that Lethe is the son of Mother Gruel (but not all of
this need have been spoken—cf. III.iv.185). Lethe must have *confess'd*
this to him.
    123. *countrymen*] see II.iii.10, note, and I.i.16–22.
    125. *honest*] chaste.
    125. *Christmas*] implying the licentious festivities of that season (Price).
    126. *bestow*] marry off.   127. *seeded*] impregnated.
    127. *good stuff*] see III.i.182, note.

Whom you have most unnaturally abus'd,
Beget your pardon.
LETHE [*aside*].   Who should that be?
Or who would do't, that has been so abus'd?   135
A troublesome penance! —[*To* Quomodo.]   Sir—
QUOMODO.
Knave in your face! Leave your mocking, Andrew;
Marry your quean and be quiet.
LETHE.   Master Easy—
EASY.
I'm sorry you take such a bad course, sir.
LETHE.
Mistress Quomodo—
THOMASINE.   Inquire my right name   140
Again next time; now go your ways like an ass
As you came.
LETHE [*aside*].
Mass, I forget my mother all this while;
I'll make her do't at first. —Pray, mother,
Your blessing for once.
MOTHER GRUEL.   Call'st me mother? Out,   145
I defy thee, slave!
LETHE.   Call me slave
As much as you will, but do not shame me now;
Let the world know you are my mother.
MOTHER GRUEL.
Let me not have this villain put upon me,
I beseech your lordship.   150
JUDGE.
He's justly curs'd; she loathes to know him now,

133–134. Whom . . . pardon] *Dyce;*   140. Mistress] *Q 2;* Maister *Q 1.*
one line in Q 1–2.   140–142. Inquire…came] *this edn.;*
134. S.D.] *this edn.*   *prose in Q 1–2.*
136. S.D.] *this edn.*   143. S.D.] *Price.*
137–138. Knave . . . quiet] *Sampson*   144–150.] *Price; prose in Q 1–2.*
(*subs.*); *prose (?) in Q 1–2.*

137. *Knave . . . face*] I call you knave to your face (Price). There may be
a pun on "merry-Andrew," a zany or clown.
140. *right name*] She still wants to be Mistress Easy.
141. *Again*] against (Dyce), in preparation for.
146. *defy*] reject, renounce (Dyce).

Whom he before did as much loathe to know.
Wilt thou believe me, woman?

MOTHER GRUEL.   That's soon done.

JUDGE.

Then know him for a villain; 'tis thy son.

MOTHER GRUEL.

Art thou Andrew, my wicked son Andrew?   155

LETHE.

You would not believe me, mother.

MOTHER GRUEL.   How art thou chang'd!
Is this suit fit for thee, a tooth-drawer's son?
This country has e'en spoil'd thee since thou cam'st hither;
Thy manners . . . better than thy clothes,
But now whole clothes, and ragged manners.   160
It may well be said that truth goes naked,
For when thou hadst scarce a shirt, thou hadst
More truth about thee.

JUDGE.

Thou art thine own affliction, Quomodo.
Shortyard we banish; 'tis our pleasure.   165

SHORTYARD.

Henceforth no woman shall complain for measure.

JUDGE.

And that all error from our works may stand,
We banish Falselight evermore the land.   [*Exeunt.*]

FINIS

158–163.] *this edn.; prose in Q 1–2.*   158. hither] *Q 2;* heather *Q 1.*

---

158. *This country*] another indication he is a Scot (Maxwell).
159.] Something has dropped out (cf. II.iii.440). Price suggests "then were," which fits both sense and meter very well.
162. *scarce a shirt*] cf. II.i.56.
166.] see I.i.85–89, note.

Appendix

Chronology

Approximate years are indicated by *, occurrences in doubt by (?).

Political and Literary Events	Life and Major Works of Middleton

1558
Accession of Queen Elizabeth I.
Robert Greene born.
Thomas Kyd born.

1560
George Chapman born.

1561
Francis Bacon born.

1564
Shakespeare born.
Christopher Marlowe born.

1570
Thomas Heywood born.*

1572
Thomas Dekker born.*
John Donne born.
Massacre of St. Bartholomew's Day.

1573
Ben Jonson born.*

1576
The Theatre, the first permanent public theater in London, established by James Burbage.
John Marston born.

1577
The Curtain theater opened.
Holinshed's *Chronicles of England, Scotland and Ireland*.

Drake begins circumnavigation of the earth; completed 1580.

1578
John Lyly's *Euphues: The Anatomy of Wit.*

1579
John Fletcher born.
Sir Thomas North's translation of Plutarch's *Lives.*

1580

Baptized at St. Lawrence in the Old Jewry, London, April 18.

1583
Philip Massinger born.

1584
Francis Beaumont born.*

1586
Death of Sir Philip Sidney.
John Ford born.

1587
The Rose theater opened by Henslowe.
Marlowe's *TAMBURLAINE*, Part I.*
Execution of Mary, Queen of Scots.
Drake raids Cadiz.

1588
Defeat of the Spanish Armada.
Marlowe's *TAMBURLAINE*, Part II.*

1589
Greene's *FRIAR BACON AND FRIAR BUNGAY.*
Marlowe's *THE JEW OF MALTA.*
Kyd's *THE SPANISH TRAGEDY.*

1590
Spenser's *Faerie Queene* (Books I–III) published.
Sidney's *Arcadia* published.
Shakespeare's *HENRY VI*, Parts I–III,* *TITUS ANDRONICUS.*

1591
Shakespeare's *RICHARD III.*

1592

Marlowe's *DOCTOR FAUSTUS**
and *EDWARD II.**
Shakespeare's *TAMING OF THE
SHREW** and *THE COMEDY OF
ERRORS.**
Death of Greene.

1593

Shakespeare's *LOVE'S LABOR'S
LOST*;* *Venus and Adonis* published.
Death of Marlowe.
Theaters closed on account of
plague.

1594

Shakespeare's *TWO GENTLE-
MEN OF VERONA*;* *The Rape of
Lucrece* published.
Shakespeare's company becomes
Lord Chamberlain's Men.
Death of Kyd.

1595

The Swan theater built.
Sidney's *Defense of Poesy* published.
Shakespeare's *ROMEO AND
JULIET,** *A MIDSUMMER
NIGHT'S DREAM,** *RICHARD
II.**
Raleigh's first expedition to
Guiana.

1596

Spenser's *Faerie Queene* (Books IV–
VI) published.
Shakespeare's *MERCHANT OF
VENICE,** *KING JOHN.**
James Shirley born.

1597

Bacon's *Essays* (first edition).
Shakespeare's *HENRY IV*, Part I.*

The Wisdom of Solomon Paraphrased
(poem).

1598

Demolition of The Theatre.
Shakespeare's *MUCH ADO
ABOUT NOTHING,** *HENRY IV*,
Part II.*

Matriculated at Queen's College,
Oxford, April 9.

Jonson's *EVERY MAN IN HIS HUMOR* (first version).
Seven books of Chapman's translation of Homer's *Iliad* published.

1599
The Paul's Boys reopen their theater.
The Globe theater opened.
Shakespeare's *AS YOU LIKE IT,* *HENRY V, JULIUS CAESAR.**
Marston's *ANTONIO AND MELLIDA*, Parts I and II.*
Dekker's *THE SHOEMAKERS' HOLIDAY.**
Death of Spenser.

Micro-Cynicon: Six Snarling Satires (poems).

1600
Shakespeare's *TWELFTH NIGHT.**
The Fortune theater built by Alleyn.
The Children of the Chapel begin to play at the Blackfriars.

The Ghost of Lucrece (poem).

1601
Shakespeare's *HAMLET,* *MERRY WIVES OF WINDSOR.**
Insurrection and execution of the Earl of Essex.
Jonson's *POETASTER.*

1602
Shakespeare's *TROILUS AND CRESSIDA.**

Married to Mary, or Magdalen, Marbeck.*
CAESAR'S FALL, with Dekker, Drayton, Munday, Webster (lost, Admiral's Men); *THE CHESTER TRAGEDY, OR RANDALL EARL OF CHESTER* (lost, Admiral's Men); *THE FAMILY OF LOVE** (Admiral's [?]); *BLURT MASTER CONSTABLE* (?) (Paul's Boys).
December 14, receives five shillings for a prologue and epilogue for a court performance of *FRIAR BACON AND FRIAR BUNGAY.*

1603

Death of Queen Elizabeth I; accession of James VI of Scotland as James I.
Florio's translation of Montaigne's *Essays* published.
Shakespeare's *ALL'S WELL THAT ENDS WELL.**
Heywood's *A WOMAN KILLED WITH KINDNESS.*
Marston's *THE MALCONTENT.**
Shakespeare's company becomes the King's Men.

*THE PHOENIX** (Paul's Boys).
The True Narration of the Entertainment of His Royal Majesty from Edinburgh till London (pamphlet).

1604

Shakespeare's *MEASURE FOR MEASURE,* OTHELLO.**
Marston's *THE FAWN.**
Chapman's *BUSSY D'AMBOIS.**

Son Edward born.*
The Ant and the Nightingale, or Father Hubburd's Tales; *The Black Book* (pamphlets).
THE HONEST WHORE, Part I, with Dekker (Prince Henry's Men); *THE PURITAN, OR THE WIDOW OF WATLING STREET* (?)* (Paul's Boys).

1605

Shakespeare's *KING LEAR.**
Marston's *THE DUTCH COURTESAN.**
Bacon's *Advancement of Learning* published.
The Gunpowder Plot.

MICHAELMAS TERM; A MAD WORLD, MY MASTERS; A TRICK TO CATCH THE OLD ONE (all acted by Paul's Boys).

1606

Shakespeare's *MACBETH.**
Jonson's *VOLPONE.**
Tourneur's *REVENGER'S TRAGEDY.**
The Red Bull theater built.
Death of John Lyly.

THE VIPER AND HER BROOD (lost).

1607

Shakespeare's *ANTONY AND CLEOPATRA.**

*YOUR FIVE GALLANTS** (Children of the Chapel).

Beaumont's *KNIGHT OF THE BURNING PESTLE.**

Settlement of Jamestown, Virginia.

1608

Shakespeare's *CORIOLANUS,** *TIMON OF ATHENS,** *PERICLES.**

Chapman's *CONSPIRACY AND TRAGEDY OF CHARLES, DUKE OF BYRON.**

Dekker's *Gull's Hornbook* published.

Richard Burbage leases Blackfriars Theatre for King's Company.

John Milton born.

*THE ROARING GIRL,** with Dekker (Prince Henry's Men).*

1609

Shakespeare's *CYMBELINE;** *Sonnets* published.

Jonson's *EPICONE.*

Sir Robert Sherley's Entertainment in Cracovia (pamphlet).

1610

Jonson's *ALCHEMIST.*

Chapman's *REVENGE OF BUSSY D'AMBOIS.**

Richard Crashaw born.

1611

Authorized (King James) Version of the Bible published.

Shakespeare's *THE WINTER'S TALE,** *THE TEMPEST.**

Beaumont and Fletcher's *A KING AND NO KING.*

Tourneur's *ATHEIST'S TRAGEDY.**

Chapman's translation of *Iliad* completed.

THE SECOND MAIDEN'S TRAGEDY (?)* (King's Men); *A CHASTE MAID IN CHEAPSIDE** (Lady Elizabeth's Men); *WIT AT SEVERAL WEAPONS*, (?)* with Rowley (unknown company).*

1612

Webster's *THE WHITE DEVIL.**

NO WIT, NO HELP LIKE A WOMAN'S (Lady Elizabeth's Men [?]).

1613

The Globe theater burned.

Shakespeare's *HENRY VIII* (with Fletcher).

Webster's *THE DUCHESS OF MALFI.**

NEW RIVER ENTERTAINMENT, September 29 (civic entertainment); *THE TRIUMPHS OF TRUTH*, October 29 (civic pageant).*

Sir Thomas Overbury murdered.

1614
The Globe theater rebuilt.
The Hope theater built.
Jonson's *BARTHOLOMEW FAIR*.

THE MASQUE OF CUPID (lost, Merchant Tailors Hall).

1615

THE WITCH* (King's Men); *MORE DISSEMBLERS BESIDES WOMEN** (King's Men).

1616
Publication of Folio edition of Jonson's *Works*.
Chapman's *Whole Works of Homer*.
Death of Shakespeare.
Death of Beaumont.

THE WIDOW (?)* (King's Men); *HENGIST, KING OF KENT** (King's Men); *THE NICE VALOR*, (?)* with Fletcher (King's Men). *CIVITATIS AMOR* (civic pageant).

1617

THE TRIUMPHS OF HONOR AND INDUSTRY (civic pageant). *A FAIR QUARREL*, with Rowley (Prince Charles' Men).

1618
Outbreak of Thirty Years War.
Execution of Raleigh.

THE OLD LAW,* with Rowley and Massinger (King's Men [?]). *The Peacemaker* (pamphlet).

1619

THE INNER TEMPLE MASQUE, OR MASQUE OF HEROES; *THE WORLD TOSSED AT TENNIS*, with Rowley (Prince Charles' Men). *THE TRIUMPHS OF LOVE AND ANTIQUITY*, October 29 (civic pageant). *On the Death of Richard Burbage* (elegy).

1620
Settlement of Plymouth, Massachusetts.

Appointed City Chronologer, September 6. *The Marriage of the Old and New Testament* (?) (pamphlet).

1621
Robert Burton's *Anatomy of Melancholy* published.

ANYTHING FOR A QUIET LIFE,* with Webster (?) (King's Men);

Andrew Marvell born.

WOMEN BEWARE WOMEN* (King's Men [?]).
THE SUN IN ARIES, with Munday (?) (civic pageant); *HONORABLE ENTERTAINMENTS* (civic entertainments).

1622
Henry Vaughan born.

THE CHANGELING, with Rowley (Lady Elizabeth's Men).
AN INVENTION FOR THE LORD MAYOR (private entertainment); *THE TRIUMPHS OF HONOR AND VIRTUE* (civic pageant).

1623
Publication of Folio edition of Shakespeare's *COMEDIES, HISTORIES, AND TRAGEDIES*.

THE SPANISH GYPSY, with Rowley (Lady Elizabeth's Men).
THE TRIUMPHS OF INTEGRITY (civic pageant).

1624

A GAME AT CHESS (King's Men).

1625
Death of King James I; accession of Charles I.
Death of Fletcher.

1626
Death of Tourneur.
Death of Bacon.

THE TRIUMPHS OF HEALTH AND PROSPERITY (civic pageant).

1627

Buried July 4 at Newington Butts.

1628
Ford's *THE LOVER'S MELANCHOLY*.
Petition of Right.
Buckingham assassinated.

1631
Shirley's *THE TRAITOR*.
Death of Donne.
John Dryden born.

1632
Massinger's *THE CITY MADAM.**

1633

Donne's *Poems* published.
Death of George Herbert.

1634

Death of Chapman, Marston, Webster.*
Publication of *THE TWO NOBLE KINSMEN*, with title-page attribution to Shakespeare and Fletcher.
Milton's *Comus*.

1635

Sir Thomas Browne's *Religio Medici*.

1637

Death of Jonson.

1639

First Bishops' War.
Death of Carew.*

1640

Short Parliament.
Long Parliament impeaches Laud.
Death of Massinger, Burton.

1641

Irish rebel.
Death of Heywood.

1642

Charles I leaves London; Civil War breaks out.
Shirley's *COURT SECRET*.
All theaters closed by Act of Parliament.

1643

Parliament swears to the Solemn League and Covenant.

1645

Ordinance for New Model Army enacted.

1646

End of First Civil War.

1647

Army occupies London.
Charles I forms alliance with Scots.

Publication of Folio edition of
Beaumont and Fletcher's *COM-
EDIES AND TRAGEDIES.*

1648
Second Civil War.

1649
Execution of Charles I.

1650
Jeremy Collier born.

1651
Hobbes' *Leviathan* published.

1652
First Dutch War began (ended
1654).
Thomas Otway born.

1653
Nathaniel Lee born.*

1656
D'Avenant's *THE SIEGE OF
RHODES* performed at Rutland
House.

1657
John Dennis born.

1658
Death of Oliver Cromwell.
D'Avenant's *THE CRUELTY OF
THE SPANIARDS IN PERU* per-
formed at the Cockpit.

1660
Restoration of Charles II.
Theatrical patents granted to
Thomas Killigrew and Sir William
D'Avenant, authorizing them to
form, respectively, the King's and
the Duke of York's Companies.

1661
Cowley's *THE CUTTER OF COLE-
MAN STREET.*
D'Avenant's *THE SIEGE OF
RHODES* (expanded to two parts).

1662
Charter granted to the Royal
Society.

1663
Dryden's *THE WILD GALLANT*.
Tuke's *THE ADVENTURES OF
FIVE HOURS*.

1664
Sir John Vanbrugh born.
Dryden's *THE RIVAL LADIES*.
Dryden and Howard's *THE
INDIAN QUEEN*.
Etherege's *THE COMICAL RE-
VENGE*.

1665
Second Dutch War began (ended
1667).
Great Plague.
Dryden's *THE INDIAN EM-
PEROR*.
Orrery's *MUSTAPHA*.

1666
Fire of London.
Death of James Shirley.